The Police in War

The Police in War

Fighting Insurgency, Terrorism, and Violent Crime

David H. Bayley
Robert M. Perito

BOULDER
LONDON

Published in the United States of America in 2010 by
Lynne Rienner Publishers, Inc.
1800 30th Street, Boulder, Colorado 80301
www.rienner.com

and in the United Kingdom by
Lynne Rienner Publishers, Inc.
3 Henrietta Street, Covent Garden, London WC2E 8LU

Library of Congress Cataloging-in-Publication Data
Bayley, David H.
The police in war : fighting insurgency, terrorism, and violent crime / by David H. Bayley and Robert M. Perito.
p. cm.
Includes bibliographical references and index.
ISBN 978-1-58826-729-0 (hbk. : alk. paper)
ISBN 978-1-58826-705-4 (pbk.: alk. paper)
1. Police—Iraq. 2. Police—Afghanistan. 3. Law enforcement—Political aspects. 4. Internal security. 5. Terrorism—Prevention. 6. Insurgency. 7. Crime prevention. 8. Postwar reconstruction—Iraq. 9. Postwar reconstruction—Afghanistan. I. Perito, Robert, 1942– II. Title.
HV8242.55.A3B39 2010
355.1'3323—dc22

2009033046

British Cataloguing in Publication Data
A Cataloguing in Publication record for this book is available from the British Library.

Printed and bound in the United States of America

The paper used in this publication meets the requirements of the American National Standard for Permanence of Paper for Printed Library Materials Z39.48-1992.

5 4 3 2 1

To
Sarah Farnham,
David's delightful granddaughter,
and
Gloria Cohan,
Bob's beloved wife

Contents

Acknowledgments

This book would not have been possible without the encouragement and timely support of the United States Institute of Peace, which provided a stimulating and productive environment for thinking and writing about peacebuilding. We are grateful to the institute's president, Richard Solomon, and to its two vice presidents, Daniel Serwer, director of the Center for Post-Conflict Peace and Stability Operations, and Pamela Aall, director of the Education and Training Center/Domestic, for their wisdom and generosity. We want to thank Nadia Gerspatcher, an expert on police issues in her own right, who integrated our work with the institute's educational program, and Madeline Kristoff, a staff member of the Center for Post-Conflict Peace and Stability Operations, who provided research support and fit the disparate pieces of our work together. USIP is devoted to resolving violent international conflicts; promoting postconflict stability; and increasing conflict management capacity, tools, and intellectual capital. We hope that this book will contribute to the achievement of those goals.

Special appreciation is also due to the School of Criminal Justice of the State University of New York at Albany for providing David Bayley with time to travel and write, as well as for its intellectual and administrative support of this effort.

In recent years, the United States and the wider international community have been engaged in stabilizing and reconstructing countries that have suffered from conflict, acute humanitarian emergencies, or failed governments. Peacebuilding interventions have become a major activity of government and a fateful one. From our involvement in many of these operations, we have developed enormous respect for the courage, dedication, and expertise of the people engaged in reconstructing postconflict societies. This book reflects the contribution of scores of these international participants: senior policymakers, mission directors, military commanders, police advisers, and police officers. They provided documentation, candid appraisals of policy, and unfailing encouragement. We are especially grateful to the many people—officials, members of NGOs, journalists, civilians—who provided perspective on the views of the recipients of international peacebuilding. Because the number of informants to whom we are indebted is easily several hundred from many countries, we won't try to list them by name. But we are grateful to all of them and hope that they will find our discussion worth their assistance. Without them, not only would our book not have been written but the world would be a sadder place.

On the purely personal side, we are grateful to our wives, Chris and Gloria, for their love and encouragement. Their wisdom, enthusiasm, and intelligence are reflected in this text.

—David H. Bayley and
Robert M. Perito

Introduction

A US Marine officer newly returned from fighting in Iraq asked us, "How should I have gone about training Iraqi police in a place where security had not been fully established, insurgent attacks were still common, and criminal gangs operated with impunity?" His unit had been faced with this task in Anbar Province after the insurgents had been suppressed through military action. He had asked for help from his chain of command, looked for information within the Department of Defense, talked to colleagues, and searched the Internet—all in vain.

This book tries to answer the marine's question—which is not unique to the operations in Iraq and Afghanistan, although we will give particular attention to those. It has troubled US-led international interventions in Somalia (1992), Haiti (1995), Bosnia-Herzegovina (1996), and Kosovo (1999). It will likely challenge US and coalition forces in future peace and stability operations.

In order to answer the question, it is necessary to address several issues implicit within it:

1. Do local police have a role in controlling violence, specifically counterinsurgency and terrorism that may persist after a peacekeeping intervention? What activities are involved?
2. What is the division of labor between the military and the police in suppressing politically destabilizing violence?
3. How should local police be trained so as to support stable, sustainable self-government?
4. Are larger governmental reforms required in order to enable local police to become effective as an instrument of democratic development?

5. Assuming that our analysis of these issues is correct, what does the US government need to do in order to improve its performance in security sector reform, police in particular, in postconflict environments?

We begin our analysis with a review of the unsuccessful US experience with police reconstruction in Iraq and Afghanistan (Chapter 1). In those operations, the dilemma of creating legitimate and effective indigenous police forces in the midst of insurgent violence has been brought sharply into focus. What went wrong? What were the problems that US forces encountered that couldn't be solved through conventional military means?

We then look back at pre–September 11 peace and stability operations since the end of the Cold War, where lessons might have been learned about appropriate training for indigenous police forces (Chapter 2). We focus on police-building in stability operations, the goal of which is to create a legitimate and effective government that can deliver essential services, including rule of law. These are missions in which the dilemma of developing effective and humane civil authority amid continuing violence is especially acute. Military-led missions of this sort have been a long-standing part of US military history, beginning in the Philippines after the Spanish-American War (1898), continuing in Central America (notably Nicaragua and Guatemala) in the early twentieth century, and culminating in the occupations of Germany and Japan following World War II. Between World War II and the end of the Cold War, Vietnam was the most protracted and difficult US counterinsurgency stabilization and reconstruction effort.

As a result of its experience in Iraq and Afghanistan, the US military recently developed a new counterinsurgency (COIN) doctrine for dealing with the sort of violence encountered in stabilization missions, whereby the ultimate objective is the establishment of an effective, sustainable local government (US Army/US Marine Corps 2006). Many of its principles had been developed in Vietnam but not incorporated into military planning and training. We review this doctrine, drawing out its implications for the development of local police (Chapter 3). In studying the role of the police in counterinsurgency, we discovered that it was remarkably similar to what has been recommended for police in coping with counterterrorism and the prevention of violent crime. In other words, across three categories of violence, we have found a strong consensus on the contribution that police can make to the control of violence.

In Chapter 4, we build on COIN doctrine by analyzing the security continuum along which peacebuilding missions are deployed, specifying the sort of police operations that are possible, as well as necessary, at different stages. We do this because, in order to determine the training that local police should receive in counterinsurgency, counterterrorism, and crime control, it is necessary to specify the functions they should perform. Roles determine training, not the other way around. This may seem blindingly obvious—but in mission after mission, whether performed under US or international leadership, training programs have been put in place like canned food that is presumed to be universally nourishing. In complex environments, however, one size doesn't fit all. Between the poles of total war and total peace, there are gradations in security that shape the police role.

Local police are not, of course, the only security force in the game. Foreign military is a given—sometimes supported by foreign police—while local military may also be present. The division of labor among all these forces also depends on a country's position along the security continuum.

Having specified what police should be trained to do in a variety of security contexts, we can answer the marine officer's question. In Chapter 5, we specify the nature, length, and modality of training that local police should receive during foreign stabilization and reconstruction. The key contribution of local police forces, we argue, is to legitimate self-government by responding under law to the security needs of individual citizens. As foreseen in contemporary COIN doctrine, police contribute uniquely in this way to winning the hearts and minds of a population for a new government. Theirs is a function that cannot be performed by military personnel, either local or foreign.

To the act of serving and protecting the local population in a manner consistent with democratic values we give the name *core policing*. Not only is it necessary for the development of stable self-government but, as shown in Chapter 3, it ensures the police are more effective in containing violence that arises variously from insurgency, terrorism, and violent crime. Core policing is an enhancer both of legitimacy and law-enforcement effectiveness. In controlling insurgency and terrorism, it is more effective to train and deploy local police to do core policing than to train them to become so-called little soldiers who support or supplement military forces in offensive counterinsurgency operations.

Unfortunately for the success of peacebuilding, officers from current police training programs in Iraq, Afghanistan, and elsewhere do not develop the unique comparative advantage of local police in combating insurgency, terrorism and violent crime. In Chapter, 6 we examine the state of training in past and current peacemaking missions, comparing them to one another and against our own recommendations. Local police training in postconflict operations is debilitated by ad hoc planning, systemic lack of documentation, and weak accountability; it is also overly militarized, focusing on the technical skills of law enforcement rather than on community service and crime prevention.

Any sort of police training designed to contribute to the development of sustainable self-government via the protection of local populations needs to be facilitated by institutional reform. Reform within police forces cannot be achieved solely through the training of frontline personnel. Effective reconstruction does not bubble up; it percolates downward. In Chapter 7, we discuss the institutional prerequisites of successful police reconstruction and development. At the same time, we examine the requirements for planning and implementing programs of this sort within missions.

In the conclusion, Chapter 8, we summarize our analysis and draw out its implications for current US efforts at stabilization and reconstruction. What steps are being taken to meet the shortcomings we have highlighted? What does the US government need to do that isn't being done?

The cruel dilemma of peacebuilding is that just as security is necessary for the development of effective civil government, so civil government is necessary for security. Violence is both a cause and an effect of failed government. What local police do to minimize violence will determine whether new governments will be regarded as worth supporting—but what police can do will be determined reciprocally by the security environment. Balancing these considerations is the challenge of peacebuilding amid violence.

1

Getting It Wrong: Iraq and Afghanistan

> *The Bush Administration has portrayed the insurgency that is roiling Iraq as an unfortunate, and unavoidable, accident of history, an enemy that emerged only after melting away during the rapid American advance toward Baghdad. The sole mistake Mr. Bush has acknowledged in the war is not foreseeing what he termed that "catastrophic success."*
> —M. Gordon (2004)

The problems of developing sustainable government through stabilization and reconstruction have been dramatically demonstrated following US military interventions in Iraq (2003) and Afghanistan (2001) after the attacks on the World Trade Towers and the Pentagon on September 11. As George W. Bush himself warned the nation during his 2000 election campaign, nation building is difficult and costly and the United States should always be cautious about undertaking it (Commission on Presidential Debates 2000). After initial military success in the overthrow of the regimes in Afghanistan and Iraq, violence against the new governments, domestic military and police, and foreign stabilization forces escalated sharply. Well-armed, well-organized insurgencies arose in both countries, killing and wounding thousands of Iraqis and Afghanis, undermining the legitimacy of local governments, raising the human and financial costs of intervention, and generating pressure for the withdrawal of donor forces.

In this chapter, we describe the US experience with stabilization and reconstruction in Iraq and Afghanistan, paying particular attention to the problems of establishing law and order. Before drawing lessons about what might be done in similar situations in the future—whether involving state failure, civil war, or humanitarian emergencies stemming from prolonged violence—it is important to understand the difficulties of security stabilization and reconstruction in all their gritty, real-world complexity.

Iraq

In planning for postconflict operations in Iraq, senior US officials in the White House and the Defense Department (DOD) assumed that coalition forces would inherit a fully functioning state with its institutions intact. They believed that the Iraqis would welcome US troops as liberators and that Iraqis would join coalition forces in quickly neutralizing the Baath Party, Saddam Hussein's security services, and other opponents of the new order (Schmitt and Sanger 2003). As National Security Advisor Condoleezza Rice said in an interview, "[We] would bring in new leadership, but we were going to keep the body in place" (Schmitt and Sanger 2003). Retired US Army General Jay Garner and the staff of the Pentagon's Office of Reconstruction and Humanitarian Affairs (ORHA), which had responsibility for planning and managing the postconflict phase of operations, supposed the Iraqi police and the regular Iraqi army would remain on duty and would assume responsibility for local security and maintain public order (Jehl 2003). This would enable coalition forces to deal with regime holdouts and pockets of military resistance. At the same time, ORHA advisers would assist Iraqi technocrats with managing government ministries, public utilities, and other institutions (Slevin and Graham 2003).

Instead, the Iraqi police and all government authority simply vanished when the US Army's Third Infantry Division reached the center of Baghdad on April 9, 2003. The special security and intelligence services and Baath Party operatives went into hiding. Police officers and members of the regular army took their weapons and went home (R. J. Smith 2003). As US military forces stood by and watched, jubilant crowds poured into the streets and began looting Baghdad's commercial district, ransacking government buildings, and pillaging residences of regime officials. Once it became clear that US soldiers were not going to intervene, public exuberance, joy at liberation, and economic opportunism quickly darkened into a systematic effort to strip the capital's stores and public institutions of everything of value. Celebratory pillaging was replaced by gangs of men armed with assault rifles and organized criminal groups that worked their way through government ministries, removing their contents, tearing out the plumbing and wiring, and then setting the buildings on fire (Shadid 2003a).

Looters ransacked Iraq's main medical center and the wards of Baghdad's hospitals, which were jammed with victims of US bomb strikes. Mobs removed patients from their beds and carried away medical equipment that was in use (Branigan and Atkinson 2003). So complete was the destruction that the International Committee of the Red Cross determined that the city's hospitals would be unable to treat the wounded under such conditions (Loeb and Graham 2003). Mobs of looters also attacked Baghdad's major cultural centers. Crowds burst into the National Museum of Antiquities, destroying and looting its irreplaceable Babylonian, Sumerian, and Assyrian collections. According to officials at UNESCO, the pillaging was the work of organized criminal gangs that bribed museum guards for the keys to the vaults holding the most valuable works of art (Andrews 2003). Looters and arsonists also attacked the Iraqi National Library and the country's principal Islamic library, destroying their priceless collections of manuscripts and archives (Burns 2003).

Following the disappearance of central authority, Iraqis were subjected to an uncontrolled wave of criminal violence. Saddam's release of 38,000 inmates from prison in late 2002 meant criminal elements were poised to take advantage of the breakdown in public order (M. R. Gordon 2003). Home invasions, robberies, muggings, and murders increased dramatically and affected all levels of society. Families were terrorized by the abductions and rapes of women and the kidnapping of children for ransom. Armed hijacking of luxury vehicles became endemic (Constable 2003). Such crimes went unreported by residents, who could find no one in authority (Leiby 2003); instead, many armed themselves, barricading their homes to protect their families from the Ali Babas, as the gangs of thieves that roamed freely were called. Baath Party members and former regime informants were gunned down in a wave of revenge killings (Brinkley 2003). By conservative estimates, 10,000 Iraqi civilians were killed in the year following the US intervention. For people accustomed to an overbearing security presence and the near absence of street crime, the loss of personal safety was particularly traumatic. Crime and the lack of personal security, more than terrorism or the insurgency, became the primary concerns of Iraqi citizens (Associated Press 2003).

Without the assistance of Iraqi security personnel, US military forces were unprepared to deal with the outburst of civilian violence and large-scale destruction that followed their arrival. The small number of US troops in Baghdad did not view looting as a military threat and had no orders to interfere (Diamond 2004). As the first unit into Baghdad, the Third Infantry Division had about 17,000 soldiers to police a city of over five million (Associated Press 2003). Moreover, it was a mechanized division whose tank crews were neither equipped nor trained to carry out patrols on foot. The lack of US response to the looting created a climate of impunity that shocked Iraqis even as it perpetuated widespread lawlessness.

US commanders explained that civil administration and postwar reconstruction were the responsibility of General Garner and the ORHA staff. Security conditions, however, prevented Garner's small advance team from reaching Baghdad until April 21, twelve days after US forces arrived in the city. The remainder of Garner's 300-member staff arrived by road from Kuwait several days later (Schmitt and Sanger 2003). Garner's plan for Iraq's reconstruction was based upon the assumption that his advisory teams would find government ministries intact. Instead, they found that seventeen of twenty-one ministries had been reduced to burned-out shells, their contents looted and their staff scattered, frightened, and demoralized (Bensahel et al. 2008, 109). ORHA had no military forces under its command to restore public order, and its requests for support were treated with indifference or disdained by US military commanders. It was also unable to rely on the types of international police forces that had contributed to peace and stability operations in Haiti, Bosnia, Kosovo, and Timor-Leste (Moss and Rohde 2006). White House and DOD officials rejected Garner's preintervention appeals for a coalition of US-led international constabulary and police forces, repeating assurances from Iraqi exiles that Americans would be welcomed with "sweets and flowers" (Rieff 2003).

Responsibility for law and order fell to coalition military forces that were neither trained nor equipped to perform police functions (Leiby 2003). US soldiers complained they had not been trained to fight crime and should not be asked to arrest offenders (Reuters 2003). In Baghdad, the Third Infantry Division's M1 tanks and Bradley Fighting Vehicles were too large to move through streets clogged with traffic. A US Army sergeant protested that it was futile for him to pursue nimble car thieves through the city's narrow alleys in his lumbering Bradley Fighting Vehicle (M. R. Gordon 2003).

The Iraqi National Police

In the aftermath of the US capture of Baghdad, the Iraqi National Police (INP) was the only institution in Saddam's network of intelligence and security services to remain intact (Coalition Provisional Authority 2003). Saddam ruled Iraq through a sophisticated structure of intelligence and security services, a vast network of informers, and the use of extreme brutality against dissenters. He skillfully balanced competing forces within the country, playing upon ethnic and religious rivalries while employing such tactics as co-optation and financial inducements. Saddam concentrated decisionmaking within a tight circle of close relatives, tribal cohorts, and fellow natives of Takrit. Beyond this ruling group, he relied upon patronage, tribal allegiance, ethnic affiliation, and economic leverage (Perito 2003).

At the bottom of the pyramid of security agencies was the INP, which was responsible for traffic control and dealing with petty crime (Moss and Rohde 2006). Established after 1920 when Iraq became a British-mandated territory, the INP operated under the Ministry of the Interior (MOI) and employed members of all ethnic groups and religious denominations. In the 1960s, police academies were established to improve training. After 1968, the Baath Party enacted legislation that subjected the police to military oversight (Coalition Provisional Authority 2003). Armed with outdated assault rifles, the INP was accustomed to relying upon the more favored special security services to perform all but the most routine operations. Thirty years of neglect by Saddam's regime had left the INP with low performance standards, poor management, and a "firehouse" mentality, whereby police officers remained in their stations until ordered to go out to make arrests (Burke 2004; Freedberg 2003). Their normal modus operandi was to round up all possible suspects, obtain confessions through brutal interrogation, and then collect bribes from family members to release those believed not guilty. In 2003, the INP consisted of 60,000 personnel, divided between an officer corps educated at the police academies and a rank and file that was poorly educated and had received little training (Coalition Provisional Authority 2003).

With looters on the streets, fires burning in government buildings, and no other recourse, US military authorities issued a public appeal for Iraqi police to return to duty. On April 14, 2003, joint patrols of US soldiers and Iraqi police tentatively made their appearance on the streets of the capital (Burns 2003). Iraqi police were not permitted to carry weapons, but even so, the presence of some officers produced outrage from citizens who claimed they were guilty of corruption and other abuses under Saddam. Like other public institutions, police infrastructure was heavily damaged and, in some places, completely destroyed by looters and arsonists following the collapse of regime authority. Rampaging mobs destroyed police stations, stole police vehicles, and walked away with weapons and equipment (Gordon and

Trainor 2007). And even with US military support, the Iraqi police were incapable of restoring public order (Ricks 2003).

As attacks by the insurgency multiplied over the summer, coalition forces increasingly relied on speed and armor, thereby reducing their contacts with local citizens. The emphasis on self-protection meant that US troops were unable to conduct foot patrols to protect Iraqi citizens from criminals, whose numbers were growing. Over time, coalition forces became increasingly insensitive to violent Iraqi-on-Iraqi crime. Commanders maintained that the Iraqi police were responsible for protecting citizens, although it was evident to Iraqis that the police could not control the lawlessness without considerable direct support from coalition forces (Sheridan 2003). The callous attitude on the part of the coalition toward the plight of Iraqi citizens accounts, in part, for the similar lack of Iraqi concern about insurgent attacks on coalition troops. The growing animosity between Iraqis and coalition troops was further exacerbated by involvement of US forces in counterinsurgency operations (Bensahel et al. 2008). Above all, the use of US combat troops to search homes, operate traffic checkpoints, and control public demonstrations created opportunities for clashes with Iraqis and reduced popular support for the Coalition Provisional Authority (CPA). In their conservative Muslim society, Iraqis complained, soldiers were entering homes without men present, addressing wives and daughters directly, and searching private areas without permission. Meanwhile, incidents of US troops dealing harshly and even firing on Iraqis increased (Shadid 2003b). Human Rights Watch reported that between June 1 and September 30, 2003, US military forces killed at least ninety-four Iraqi civilians in Baghdad at checkpoints and during house raids (Human Rights Watch 2003). Since US activity was concentrated in Sunni areas, insults, abuse, and violations of local codes of honor increased the number of those who were prepared to join the Sunni-based insurgency.

The US Police Assistance Program

In May 2003, a police assessment team from the Department of Justice's (DOJ) International Criminal Investigative Training Assistance Program (ICITAP) formally concluded that the Iraqi police were incapable of maintaining public order and would require international assistance. The team called for the deployment of over 6,600 international police advisers, including 360 professional police trainers that would be assigned to the police academy and other training sites and

170 advisers on border control functions (Moss and Rohde 2006). The mission also recommended the provision of ten fully equipped and armed international constabulary units with a total of 2,500 personnel to assist coalition military forces with restoring stability and training Iraqi counterparts (Coalition Provisional Authority 2003). This civilian security force would be consistent with the size and composition of international constabulary and police forces deployed in Haiti, Bosnia, Kosovo, and Timor-Leste. Numbers were understated in relationship to actual needs, but they represented the concerns of experienced professionals regarding the security challenge and their serious doubts about donor commitment and the availability of international personnel.

The assessment team's report was discussed at White House meetings in June 2003, but the recommendations were considered overly ambitious and were denied. A State Department effort to recruit one thousand US police advisers as part of the larger international police force was suspended because of a lack of funds and not resumed until late fall. The advisers, who were recruited and trained by DynCorp International under a State Department contract, did not begin arriving in Iraq in substantial numbers until the spring of 2004 (Bensahel et al. 2008). By then, the target number of advisers had been reduced to 500 because of limited funds (Moss and Rohde 2006). Though they were armed for self-defense, they did not have executive authority to engage in law enforcement. Instead they were assigned to provide leadership training and train-the-trainer programs in secure locations, as it had become too dangerous for them to mentor Iraqi police in the field. By June 2004, only 283 US police advisers had deployed, as repeated rocket and car bomb attacks on their Baghdad hotel and the deteriorating security situation in other cities discouraged volunteers (Moss 2006). The remainder of the international civil police and the entire constabulary force, which were to come from other coalition members, never materialized.

Though the US advisory team was well informed, all its hard work and determination could not compensate for the failure to foresee the collapse of Iraqi security services and the resulting breakdown in public order. Meeting the goals set by the CPA would have required a massive infusion of funds, a substantial international police force, and a large cadre of international police development experts armed with a comprehensive plan for reforming the MOI and the INP, which was renamed the Iraqi Police Service (IPS). Lack of preparation meant planning and implementation had to occur simultaneously. By December 2003, the number of international advisers assigned to the MOI had risen to only twenty-four, of which twelve were normally present at any one time. Armed with a dozen computers, this small group was asked to support the IPS, the Facilities Protection Corps, the Border Patrol, and emergency services as well as to recruit over 200,000 Iraqi personnel. During the critical first nine months of the US intervention, the small group of US police advisers operated with little funding and a minimum of interest from the CPA leadership (Hines 2004). Only after the security situation began to seriously deteriorate did the police begin to receive funds and high-level attention.

The advisers' leadership also could not compensate for the massive loss of management skills resulting from de-Baathification. The CPA's decision to ban ranking Baath Party members from public sector employment affected large numbers of senior officers in the MOI, police, and security-related services who were apolitical but had become party members as a condition of employment (Burke 2004). In previous peace and stability operations, officials had been vetted on an individual basis and those with good records were permitted to serve. Mass firing of senior officers removed an entire executive layer whose leadership and managerial skills would have been useful in rebuilding the IPS and confronting crime and the insurgency (Waldman 2003). This action seemed not only unwise but also unfair to Iraqi police and their US advisers, particularly where the Iraqi police officers in question were making a positive contribution. In several cases, US advisers attempted to challenge the dismissal of critically needed, skilled personnel, but these efforts were generally unsuccessful (Dunford 2004).

The DOJ and the Transition Integration Program

During the summer of 2003, US Department of Justice police advisers developed a program for retraining former members of the INP, using US military police as instructors. Some 40,000 members of the IPS received up to three weeks of instruction under the police Transition and Integration Program (TIP) on the subjects of human rights, ethics and law, the use of force in making arrests, and weapons handling (Waldman 2003). TIP also endeavored to verify the identity and review the records of serving police officers, remove those who were guilty of abuses, and single out those who would benefit from additional training. Underfunded and inadequately staffed, it fell short of its modest goals but likely did convey some understanding of the nature of policing in a democratic society (Burke 2004). Many of the rehired police were disciplined or eventually dismissed from service because of identity theft, corruption, lack of formal education, or lack of police experience.

In December 2003, the US State Department and DOJ opened a basic training program for Iraqi police recruits at the Jordan International Police Training Center in Amman (Cha 2003). In the first twelve months, some 30,000 Iraqis were brought to the facility on US military flights and returned to Iraq after eight weeks of training. Recruits were selected with minimal vetting (Broadwell 2005). The curriculum, which was tailored for Iraqi students, was based on the twenty-week basic training course given at the Kosovo Police Service School and the program utilized members of the administrative staff and instructors from Kosovo (OSCE [Organization for Security and Cooperation in Europe] Mission in Kosovo 2003). When in full operation, the center graduated 2,500 police—a force the size of the Boston Police Department—every month. Once back in Iraq, newly minted officers received little or no additional mentoring or training. An effort to create a field training program using the US police advisers provided by DynCorp was abandoned after a few months because of security considerations.

The rapid infusion of tens of thousands of new IPS officers overwhelmed the CPA, which continued to use routine US government contracting, hiring, and procurement procedures for obtaining the vehicles, uniforms, weapons, and equipment needed by the IPS. Although billions of dollars were earmarked for the IPS from the fiscal 2004 US supplemental budget, donor contributions, and other sources, procedures developed for use by the Pentagon in Washington proved extremely slow and cumbersome in response to immediate needs. The small group of US police advisers was forced to improvise constantly to obtain needed equipment and supplies, but ad hoc arrangements failed to satisfy critical requirements (Burke 2004). By the spring of 2004, the IPS had received less than half of the weapons, vehicles, communications equipment, and body armor they required. Reconstruction and the refurbishment of provincial police headquarters, police stations, and regional training facilities were also behind schedule. Complaints about inadequate procedures and recommendations for improvements were lost in the constant shuffle and turnover of CPA administrative personnel. The appointment of eager but inexperienced staff to middle management and contracting positions negatively impacted all aspects of CPA operations but particularly security sector reform (Burke 2004).

The DOD and the Civilian Police Advisory Training Team

As the US-determined deadline for the transfer to Iraqi sovereignty approached, the DOD concluded that only the US military had the resources required to handle the police train and equip program. In May 2004, President George W. Bush signed a National Security Presidential Decision Directive that formally transferred responsibility for the program from the State Department to the DOD (US National Security Council 2004). In Iraq, a Civilian Police Advisory Training Team (CPATT) was established under control of the Multi-National Force—Iraq (later the Multi-National Security Transition Command—Iraq or MNSTC-I) and assigned responsibility for training, equipping, and mentoring the IPS. CPATT was led by a British brigadier general with a US civilian deputy and included both military and civilian personnel. The transfer of responsibility for civilian police training to the US military was unprecedented. In all previous peace operations, the police assistance program had been led by the State and Justice Departments (Magnier and Efron 2004). Unfortunately, the transfer was not accompanied by a meeting of the minds on such critical issues as the IPS's mission, including its relationship to US military forces and its role in countering the insurgency.

DOJ civilian police advisers and the US military had markedly different goals for the IPS. The advisers believed the military did not understand either the ethos or the practical requirements for training law enforcement officers and was intent on simply putting Iraqi guns on the street in order to reduce the pressure on coalition forces. DOJ civilian police trainers wanted to create an efficient, lightly armed, civilian police service that utilized community-policing techniques and operated in conformity with Western democratic standards of professional law enforcement. They argued that Iraq's security problems were best resolved by relying on investigations and arrests to remove criminals and terrorists. As we have noted, the curriculum at the DOJ-run police training facility in Amman was based on the training program developed for the police in Kosovo. The Kosovo program entailed two months of classroom instruction and three months of follow-up field training (OSCE Mission in Kosovo 2003); the Iraq program was reduced to ten weeks of class work and no field training (Perito 2005). Moreover, the Iraq insurgency meant that the basic assumptions of the Kosovo-based training did not apply.

Iraqi police who were trained and equipped for community policing were utilized as an auxiliary force to fight the insurgency. (The numbers of supposedly trained police were virtually meaningless as they included personnel who were prepared for a different mission.) The Iraqi police were provided with new sidearms—which were, however, useless against insurgents armed with military weapons. In short, poorly led, ill-trained, and improperly equipped police were pitted against a heavily armed insurgent force of former military personnel, veteran security operatives, and foreign terrorists. Moreover, no civilian police force could be expected to deal with repeated attacks from car bombs and forces equipped with rocket-propelled grenades and other military weapons (Al-Anbaki 2004). Involvement in the battle against insurgents also turned the police into a primary target for terrorist attacks aimed at breaking their resolve and demonstrating the danger of cooperating with the coalition (Magnier and Efron 2004). The police operated from unprotected facilities, patrolled in thin-skinned vehicles, lacked body armor, and faced increasingly grievous casualties. From 2004 to 2006, they suffered 12,000 casualties—including 4,000 killed, and 8,000 wounded—according to General Joseph Peterson, the US commander in charge of police training in Iraq (CNN World Service 2006).

For its part, the US military was determined to create indigenous security forces that could protect the Iraqi government from its internal enemies, the insurgency, and hostile militias and thus permit the withdrawal of US forces. To confront the growing insurgency, the US military created so-called heavy police units composed of former Iraqi soldiers. The original Public Order Battalion, Mechanized Police Unit, and Emergency Response Unit were composed of unvetted Sunni personnel, who were given military weapons and counterinsurgency training. In early 2006, the MNSTC-I combined these units into a constabulary force called the Iraqi National Police (INP) (Perito 2006). Under the Iraqi Interim Government, however, Interior Minister Bayan Jabr—a Shiite political leader—permitted Shiite officials to purge Sunnis and create police commando units of fighters from Shiite militia organizations (Moss 2006). By summer 2006, it had become clear that these INP units were engaged in sectarian violence and death squad activities (Perito 2007).

In December 2006, the "Year of the Police" that had been proclaimed by the US military ended with the completion of the MNSTC-I's program to train and equip 135,000 members of the IPS (US Department of Defense 2007). Training and equipment were also provided to the 24,400 members of the INP and 28,400 members of the border police. Nearly 180 US Police Transition Teams (PTTs) and thirty-nine National Police Transition Teams were embedded with Iraqi forces, while a 100-member Ministry Transition Team was assigned to the MOI to improve its operations (US Department of Defense 2007).

The achievement of these quantitative goals, while impressive, masked the troubling reality of the loyalty and quality of Iraqi police forces. In its December 2005 report, the Iraq Study Group (ISG), chaired by former Secretary of State James Baker and former House International Relations Committee Chairman Lee Hamilton, concluded that the state of the Iraqi police was substantially worse than that of the Iraqi Army. The IPS had neither the training nor the equipment to conduct criminal investigations; it also lacked the firepower to confront organized crime and was unable to protect Iraq citizens from insurgent attacks. Meanwhile, as we have mentioned, the INP routinely engaged in sectarian violence, including the illegal detention of Sunnis, torture, and executions. The Iraqi Interior Ministry, which supervised police forces, was not merely dysfunctional but also corrupt and heavily infiltrated by Shiite militias. The border police were unable to stop the movement of terrorists, arms, and contraband across Iraq's porous borders. All Iraqi police units were usually at half of their authorized strength due to attrition, chronic absenteeism, and the corrupt practice of including *ghosts* (or fictitious personnel) on the rolls. Officers often colluded with or were intimidated by insurgents, militias, and criminals. The ISG recommended transferring responsibility for training the IPS from the DOD to the DOJ and embedding US civilian police officers with Iraqi police units (Baker and Hamilton 2006).

Nearly a year later, the US effort to create an effective Iraqi police force had made some progress but still faced substantial challenges. According to the September 2007 report of the congressionally mandated Independent Commission on the Security Forces of Iraq, the IPS was improving but was still years away from making a substantial contribution to Iraqi security and protecting Iraqi neighborhoods from insurgents and sectarian violence. The commission pointed out that the IPS was incapable of conducting investigations or performing most police functions and was insufficiently equipped to face heavily armed insurgent groups and militia forces. It also noted that only 40 to 70 percent of the officers trained by the US were currently serving in the IPS—and that more precise estimates were impossible because of the aforementioned corrupt practice of ghost payrolls. In addition, tens of thousands of police who had not entered the US train and equip program had nonetheless been recruited by provincial authorities.

As for the INP, the commission believed that it was not a viable organization because of sectarianism, public distrust, and confusion over whether it was a military or police force. It noted that the INP had inadequate leadership and that its ranks were increasingly illiterate even as they remained 85 percent Shia, recruited from Iraq's southern provinces (Independent Commission on the Security Forces of Iraq 2007). The US military leadership of the training effort had militarized the INP and marginalized the US civilian police trainers. To correct this situation, the commission recommended that future training include a far larger number of senior US civilian law enforcement officers and that the role of military personnel should be reduced to providing force protection (Independent Commission on the Security Forces of Iraq 2007).

The US failure to establish a functioning Iraqi police force undermined the goal of providing a secure environment for Iraqi civilians and jeopardized the safety of the officers themselves. In terms of human suffering, this failure was catastrophic. According to conservative estimates, between 87,000 and 95,000 Iraqi civilians died from insurgent attacks or sectarian violence and hundreds of thousands were injured between March 19, 2003, and August 22, 2008 (Iraq Body Count). In addition, nearly three million Iraqis were internally displaced as a result of ethnic cleansing, while an additional two million became international refugees, mostly in Syria and Jordan (US Government Accountability Office 2008).

Afghanistan

The unilateral failure to create an effective civilian police force in Iraq was paralleled by a multilateral but equally unsuccessful effort to train and equip an effective civilian police force in Afghanistan. From a standing start in 2002, the Afghan National Police (ANP) grew to 68,000, the target end strength being 86,000. The ANP included several distinct entities operating under the direction of the MOI. These police forces included the Afghan Uniform Police, which was responsible for general police duties, and four specialized police organizations: the Afghan National Civil Order Police (ANCOP), the Afghan Border Police, the Counter Narcotics Police of Afghanistan and the Counter Terrorism Police.

The starting point for rebuilding the Afghanistan police was the Agreement on Provisional Arrangements in Afghanistan Pending Re-establishment of Permanent Institutions, otherwise known as the Bonn Agreement, signed by representatives of the Afghan people on December 5, 2001 (UN Secretariat 2001). The agreement established the Afghan Interim Authority to run the country and provided the basis for an interim system of law and governance. In Annex I, the parties called for the deployment of an international military force to maintain security in Kabul. In response, UN Security Council Resolution 1386 of December 20, 2001, authorized the creation of the International Security Assistance Force (ISAF) to assist the new Afghan government for six months (UN Security Council 2001). The ISAF deployed in January 2002 and by summer had 5,000 troops from nineteen countries. Unlike the US-led Operation Enduring Freedom, which operated along the Pakistani border and focused on destroying the Taliban and Al-Qaida, the mission of the ISAF was limited to providing security in the capital by conducting routine patrols with local police (Henry L. Stimson Center 2002, 2).

Indeed, the UN sought to limit international involvement in Afghanistan as much as possible and to encourage the Afghans to assume responsibility for their own political reconciliation, economic reconstruction, and security. Under the leadership of Ambassador Lakhdar Brahimi, the UN mission in Kabul advocated a "light footprint," or minimal international oversight and material assistance, particularly with respect to internal security and police assistance (Consortium for Response to the Afghanistan Transition 2002, 10–14). The Bonn Agreement did not provide a role for the UN in monitoring or training the Afghan police, and the Security Council did not authorize a UN police mission. According to the Bonn Agreement, responsibility for maintaining security throughout the country rested with the Afghans (UN Secretariat 2001).

Instead of taking a comprehensive approach to security sector reform, international donors adopted a so-called lead-nation framework at the 2002 G8 conference in Geneva. The security sector was divided into five pillars, with a lead nation assigned to each pillar to oversee and support reforms. Under this plan, the United States was assigned responsibility for the military, Germany for the police, Italy for the judiciary, and Britain for counternarcotics. The framework was meant to ensure burden sharing, but assignments were made with little attention to expertise, experience, or resources, and there was no mechanism to ensure a coordinated approach to reform efforts. Some donors presumed the Afghan government would assume an oversight role despite its obvious shortfalls in required capacity.

Once engaged, international donors, including the United States, regressed into instituting train and equip programs that focused on rapidly improving the operational effectiveness of Afghan security forces while largely ignoring the need to improve the effectiveness of management and governance structures. There was no effort to create an integrated framework for security sector reform. None of the donors focused on the need to strengthen the Afghan institution—the MOI—that would be responsible for overseeing and supporting the Afghan police. The German police assistance mission assigned only one adviser to the MOI in 2003. At the time, the ministry lacked basic administrative systems for personnel, procurement, and logistics, never mind the ability to oversee police operations. In short, the initial failure to dedicate sufficient effort to the reform of the MOI stifled efforts to remake the ANP (Sedra 2008, 193–196).

The Afghan Police

In the 1960s and 1970s, both the Federal Republic of Germany and the German Democratic Republic worked in Afghanistan to provide police development assistance. During the Soviet intervention, the Afghan police were organized according to the Soviet model, with a two-track system of career officers and short-term conscripts who served for two years as patrolmen as an alternative to joining the military. Officers were educated at a police academy; conscripts were untrained and often mistreated by their superiors. The police were militarized and included a light infantry force. During the subsequent civil war between mujahid commanders and the period of Taliban rule, there was no national civilian police force in Afghanistan (Wilder 2007, 3). By 2002, there were an estimated 50,000 men working as police, but they were untrained, ill equipped, and illiterate (70–90 percent), and they owed their allegiance to warlords and local commanders rather than the central government. Many were former mujahidin whose experience of acting with impunity badly prepared them to serve as police in a democratic society. A few professional police officers remained from the ANP of the Soviet period, but their training and experience were also inappropriate for the new order (Murray 2007, 109).

The Afghan Interim Authority, particularly Interior Minister Mohammed Yunus Qanooni, recognized that further international assistance would be required to revamp the Afghan National Police. It wanted to create a new professional police service with educated officers and trained, career noncommissioned officers (NCOs) and patrolmen. As we have noted, based upon their positive experiences with German police assistance prior to the Soviet intervention, the Afghans, with UN support, asked Germany to be the lead nation in training and equipping the Afghan police. Germany's goal was to create an ethnically balanced force that was familiar with human rights standards and modern police methods and would be capable of operating in a democratic society (UN Secretariat 2002, 9–12). Given Afghanistan's size and population, creating a national police force represented a far greater challenge than anything the international community had attempted in peace operations in Haiti and the Balkans.

The Germans developed an initial plan for training the Afghan police based upon the European model of police academies, providing a university-level education for officers and a shorter academic program for NCOs (Amnesty International 2003, 18). They committed US$70 million toward the renovation of the police academy in Kabul, providing eleven police instructors, refurbishing Kabul police stations, and donating fifty police vehicles. The first team of German police advisers arrived in Kabul on March 16, 2002, and the German Coordination Office was opened on March 18. The Coordination Office supervised the reconstruction of the police academy, which formally reopened on August 22, 2002, with 1,500 officer cadets enrolled in a five-year program (Government of Germany 2002). According to an interview we conducted with an official from the US State Department on April 14, 2002, the Kabul Police Academy also offered a three-month recruit course for 500 NCOs. Interior Minister Qanooni announced that the goal of the Interim Authority was to create a police force of 70,000 officers (Struck 2002). The German approach would have taken decades to train a police force of that size—if success were possible at all.

The US Police Assistance Program

The United States did not challenge the German approach to police training as inappropriate for Afghanistan. Instead, in 2003, the State Department took the more diplomatic tack of creating a separate program to provide what it called in-service training to those who were currently serving in police roles, in Kabul, where it established a training center that served as a prototype for seven regional training centers eventually constructed around the country. The State Department's Bureau of International Narcotics and Law Enforcement Affairs (State/INL) led the US police assistance program, but training center construction, instructor recruitment, and project management was contracted to DynCorp, which had played a similar role in the Balkans.

At the flagship facility in Kabul, three US and six non-US foreign instructors, along with some Afghans, handled training. Trainees were selected by the MOI and were not vetted by US program administrators (Sedra 2008, 201–202). The program offered three core courses based on a curriculum that was used at the Police Service School in Kosovo: an eight-week course in basic police skills for literate NCOs and patrolmen, a five-week course for illiterate patrolmen and a fifteen-day TIP for policemen with extensive experience. The training centers also offered a two-to-four week course in instructor development. The result was a sizable increase in the number of Afghan police with some training, reaching a total of 71,147 by July 2007 (Sedra 2008, 201–202).

The quality of the training received by the majority of the graduates of the US program is, however, open to question. Contract instructors faced a formidable challenge insofar as trainees had little or no previous classroom experience. They sat on hard benches for hours a day in prefabricated classrooms that baked in the summer and froze in the winter, listening to English-speaking instructors and their poorly trained Afghan translators, who were largely unfamiliar with police terminology. Few of the US instructors were professional police trainers, and there was little or no use of adult learning techniques. Since more than 70 percent of the Afghan trainees were illiterate, most received the five-week course for illiterate patrolmen. Recruits unable to read and write were less able to absorb information or learn such basic police skills as taking statements from witnesses, writing incident reports, and maintaining records (Murray 2007).

Trainees also did not remain at the training centers long enough to absorb the ethos of democratic policing, nor did they receive the type of follow-up field training that had been a feature of similar US programs in Panama, Haiti, and the Balkans. Instead they were returned to their place of origin with no concern for whether they were applying their training or employing the uniforms, equipment, or weapons that had been issued upon completion of the program. Many were assigned to static guard duty or reduced to serving under untrained and corrupt leaders who possessed little understanding of the role of police in a democratic society (Glanz and Rohde 2006).

In addition to training problems, the international police assistance program suffered from a lack of overarching strategic objectives, coordination between the US and German programs, poor leadership from the supervising Interior Ministry, and inadequate funding. In May 2002, the UN Development Programme established the Law and Order Trust Fund for Afghanistan (LOTFA) to enable donors to contribute funds for police salaries. By 2004, only US$11.2 million of the US$65 million requested had been contributed. The shortfall meant the Afghan government could not support the deployment of national police outside the capital. Even in Kabul, Afghan police went unpaid for months—a situation that resulted in petty corruption and thereby undermined the confidence of the public, who regarded the Afghan police with a mixture of fear and disdain (Miller and Perito 2004).

DOD and the Combined Security Transition Command

In 2005, the US government transferred responsibility for its police assistance program from the State Department to the DOD, following the lead of its program in Iraq. Implementation was assigned to the Combined Security Transition Command–Afghanistan (CSTC-A), which also had responsibility for training the Afghan National Army (ANA). Within CSTC-A, responsibility for training was assigned to the Task Force Police Directorate while responsibility for reforming the MOI went to the Police Reform Directorate. Although CSTC-A had overall responsibility, State/INL retained contract management authority for police training, mentoring, and ministry reform. State/INL also continued to provide civilian police trainers and advisers through its contract with DynCorp (Wilder 2007).

As in Iraq, the transfer of responsibility to the DOD ensured greater manpower and financial resources but did little to improve the effectiveness of the US police assistance program. In December 2006, a joint report by the inspector generals of both the State Department and the DOD found that US-trained Afghan police were incapable of conducting routine law enforcement and that program managers could account neither for the number of ANP on duty nor the whereabouts of vehicles, equipment, and weapons provided to the Afghan government. The report noted that the official figure of 70,000 trained police officers was inflated and that only about 30,000 were actually on duty and able to carry out police functions. The report faulted the lack of a central field-training program that could provide mentoring for graduates from the regional field-training centers and keep track of equipment. Despite the US$1.1 billion that had to-date been spent on police assistance in Afghanistan, the report noted that the program was understaffed, poorly supervised, and ineffective (Inspectors General, US Department of State, and US Department of Defense 2006).

In November 2007, the CSTC-A sought to correct for deficiencies in the US police training program by launching a new initiative called Focused District Development (FDD), which aimed to enhance ANP capabilities by training all uniformed police in a single district at one time as a unit. While the district police were in training, a highly skilled ANCOP unit replaced them, providing a model for local citizens of effective police performance. The FDD was designed to counter the ineffectiveness of the previous approach. Under it, an advance team of US military and civilian police advisers conducted a pretraining assessment in the district, noting the level of police infrastructure and performance, the relationship with the population, and the threat from criminals and insurgents. The entire district force was brought to a regional training center, where untrained recruits received basic training, more experienced police got advanced training, and officers underwent management and leadership training.

The FDD program included seven weeks of instruction in military tactics, weapons use, survival strategies, and counterinsurgency operations, as well as one week of training in basic police skills. While in training, the police received new uniforms and weapons, vetted leadership, and increased salaries. They were then redeployed to their district under the supervision of a US police mentoring team (US Government Accountability Office 2009). Their instructors returned with them and remained there until the Afghan police could operate without supervision. The embedded mentoring team of instructors included two civilian police advisers, four military support personnel, and a six-member military security force. It was able to work with individual officers, establishing personal relationships, providing role models, offering on-the-job training, and assessing their progress toward the independent conduct of police operations. Units were evaluated on a variety of competencies, including equipment accountability, formal training, crime handling procedures, and the use of force. Initially the mentoring teams engaged in intensive training but then pulled back to providing oversight, as the Afghans exhibited greater competence in conducting operations (US Institute of Peace, Security Sector Reform Working Group 2009).

Despite the US government's expenditure of US$6.2 billion on police assistance, a Government Accountability Office (GAO) report in June 2008 noted that according to the CSTC-A's rating system, no ANP units—which had a combined total of 70,000 personnel—were fully capable of performing their mission; nearly two-thirds of the units received the lowest capability rating. The major reasons for this shortfall were judged to be (1) the inability of the US military to provide more than 32 percent of the required military mentors (although 540 of 551 civilian police mentors were present); (2) the failure of the ANP to receive, account for, and maintain critical equipment, including weapons, vehicles, and body armor; (3) widespread corruption; (4) consistent problems with pay and administrative support; and (5) increasing attacks by insurgents (Johnson 2008).

In January 2009, the ANP in fifty-two of Afghanistan's 365 police districts were undergoing the FDD process. The CSTC-A initially projected that the entire training cycle would take up to nine months. Only four of the first seven units trained reached proficiency in ten months, and it appeared that most units would likewise require more time to complete the training cycle. In addition, the CSTC-A lacked the additional 1,500 military support and security officers required to staff the hundreds of district and provincial training teams that would be needed to complete the training of all units by the target date of December 2010. In April 2009, President Barack Obama announced the imminent deployment of 4,000 additional soldiers to train Afghan military and police forces. The chairman of the Joint Chiefs of Staff, Admiral Michael Mullen, stated that the trainers "were at the heart of building Afghanistan security forces as quickly as possible" (Gilmore 2009).

The Challenges of Drugs and the Taliban

But the failure to develop an effective Afghan police force was due not only to deficiencies in the US train and equip program; the explosion of Afghan opium production and the return of the Taliban were also factors. Starting in 2002, the Afghan government, with the assistance of the UN Office on Drugs and Crime, put in place the basic legal and institutional framework for a counternarcotics program. In January of that year, President Hamid Karzai issued a presidential decree outlawing the production, trafficking, and abuse of narcotics. In October, a Counter Narcotics Directorate was created as part of the

National Security Council. In May 2003, a National Drug Control Strategy was adopted, and in October 2003 a modern narcotics control law was enacted. Yet by 2004, opium cultivation had already spread from the traditional growing areas in the south to all of Afghanistan's thirty-two provinces. By 2006, Afghanistan had become the world's largest producer of opium, accounting for 92 percent of global production. Income earned by farmers, middlemen, processors, traffickers, and drug exporters equaled two-thirds of Afghanistan's legal gross domestic product. Revenue from opium sales financed the broad expansion of the country's already well-organized criminal networks, which stretched into Pakistan and other neighboring states. It also strengthened the power of tribal leaders, warlords, the Taliban, Al-Qaida and other Islamist extremists opposed to the US-backed government (UN Office on Drugs and Crime and Afghan Ministry of Counternarcotics 2006).

As we have noted, the UK had assumed responsibility for directing counternarcotics activity at the 2002 G8 conference in Geneva. Although well intentioned, Britain's initial efforts suffered from limited funding and inexperience and were, in some cases, counterproductive (Miller and Perito 2004, 14). Thus, the UK's lead-nation status notwithstanding, the United States emerged in 2005 as the largest international donor to and leading force in the counternarcotics efforts in Afghanistan, providing US$782 million during fiscal year 2005 for assistance in law enforcement, crop eradication, and the creation of alternative livelihood programs (US Government Accountability Office 2006). One major US initiative involved the creation of several specialized counternarcotics police forces. The Counter Narcotics Police of Afghanistan (CNPA) was established in late 2004 to conduct investigations and enforce the law. It included a National Interdiction Unit, which conducted raids throughout Afghanistan. Other counternarcotics entities in the MOI included the Central Eradication Planning Cell, which provided intelligence, and the Afghanistan Eradication Force, which engaged in on-the-ground destruction of poppy fields. Separate from the CNPA was the Afghanistan Special Narcotics Force, which reported directly to the president and the interior minister and which carried out interdiction missions against high-value targets (Inspectors General, US Department of State, and US Department of Defense 2006, 12).

Though the stepped-up, US-led counternarcotics effort had only limited impact on the manufacture of Afghan opium and heroin, which hit record levels in 2007, production did fall by 6 percent in

2008 largely as a result of drought on the one hand and oversuppply on the other. In its *Afghanistan Opium Survey 2008,* the UN Office of Drugs and Crime reported that Afghanistan remained the world's largest producer of illicit drugs (UN Office of Drugs and Crime and Afghan Ministry of Counternarcotics 2008). The report noted that the seven southwestern provinces that form the Taliban's base of operations accounted for 66 percent of Afghanistan's opium production—an increase from 2007. According to the executive director of the UN Office of Drugs and Crime, the Taliban earned between US$200 million and US$400 million through a 10 percent tax on opium growers and drug traffickers operating in areas under its control in exchange noninterference in the illicit trade (Lynch 2008). The link between the insurgency and the drug trade was demonstrated in May 2009 when a four-day battle that killed sixty insurgents in Helmand Province also resulted in the confiscation of 101 tons of heroin, opium, hashish, and processing materials, the largest drug seizure by US and Afghan forces to date (Tavernise 2009, 9).

Beyond funding the Taliban, the revenue from opium production fueled widespread corruption that affected all levels of the Afghan government, including its ministries and parliament. The nearly universal belief among Afghans that officials in the MOI, provincial police chiefs, and members of the ANP alike were involved in the drug trade diminished public confidence and respect for the police. This belief was based on widespread reports of senior MOI officials accepting large bribes for protecting drug traffickers and assigning senior provincial and district police positions to persons engaged in the drug trade (Jones et al. 2006, 119). A combination of local loyalties, links to criminal networks, lack of incentive due to low salary (or, often, no salary), and a residual culture of impunity contributed to endemic corruption in the ANP.

In many communities, ANP officers were viewed as predatory, posing a greater threat to security than the Taliban with their demands for bribes, illegal taxes, and various kinds of human rights violations. They were also known to use house searches as an opportunity to shake down the occupants and steal their possessions. Corrupt police practices were felt most directly by the poorest members of society: taxi and truck drivers, traders, small businessmen, and farmers. Furthermore, it was not uncommon for police officers to pay bribes to their superiors in exchange for unjustified promotions and/or assignments that would allow them to engage in extortion and smuggling. The embezzlement of official funds and the theft of gasoline for sale on the black market were also common, as was the use of ghost payrolls by police chiefs, who skimmed the funds thereby made available (Oppel 2009). Police officers even sold weapons and ammunition to criminals and the Taliban. Such corruption not only eroded public support for the police but also severely undermined the legitimacy of the Afghan government (Sarway 2008).

Drug abuse by police was increasingly common as well, particularly in drug-producing areas such as Helmand Province. According to the UK Foreign Office, an estimated 60 percent of the Afghan police in Helmand used drugs, which further undermined security and contributed to official corruption. Nationwide, according to UK narcotics experts, 16 percent of Afghan police tested positive for narcotics use in 2008 (Australian Broadcasting Company 2009).

The Return of the Taliban

The initial decision to restrict the ISAF's mission to the patrol of Kabul meant that UN officials and other international assistance providers were also largely restricted to the capital and its environs and were unable to function in other areas of the country. Meanwhile, extremist groups—namely the Taliban, Al-Qaida, and Hezb-i-Islami—began to establish themselves in sanctuaries across the border in Pakistan, where they focused on recruiting followers and rebuilding their organizations. When these groups returned to Afghanistan in force in 2004, they benefited from the lack of a central government presence and continued disorder in the border regions. Afghans living in these critical areas were committed neither to the central government or the US-led coalition and had little reason to resist the insurgents (Dobbins 2008, 7).

Over the next three years, insurgent activity both increased in frequency and spread throughout the country. As Operation Enduring Freedom doubled its forces in 2005, the Taliban shifted its tactics from attacking coalition forces to targeting Afghan civilians and representatives of humanitarian organizations. By 2007, the Taliban was relying increasingly on terrorism, ambushes, and small unit attacks, conducting over 140 suicide bombings, many of them in Kabul. The Taliban was most active, however, in its traditional strongholds in the south, where the central government remained weak and unable to provide governance and public services (Jones and Pickering 2008, 23). In 2008, public opinion polls showed that Afghans considered the absence of public security in the face of insurgent attacks, criminal robberies, abductions, murders, and tribal violence to be the nation's primary problem (S. Jones 2006, 113–114).

ANP officers who worked in their own communities formed the frontline defense against terrorism and the insurgency and therefore bore the brunt of the violence. Beyond being inadequately trained and ill equipped, they were poorly led and inappropriately used to fight heavily armed insurgents (Jalali 2009). To quote one Afghan officer, "Firing rockets is not the job of police" (Nelson 2009). The ANP accompanied coalition and ANA patrols and were expected to operate as "little soldiers," helping to seize and hold territory and prevent the return of the Taliban. According to the MOI's National Internal Security Strategy, coalition forces, the ANA, and the ANP "continue to wage war against armed groups" (Afghan Ministry of Interior 2006). Police were used to man isolated checkpoints and establish a government presence in rural villages. Operating in small groups with no means of communication and no backup, they were no match for insurgent groups that targeted their convoys, checkpoints, and bases (US Institute of Peace, Security Sector Reform Working Group 2009).

The cost of using police in a combat role for which they were never intended has been extremely high. According to the DOD, some 3,400 Afghan police were killed or wounded between January 2007 and March 2009. Police combat losses in 2008 were three times greater than those of the ANA, with an average of fifty-six casualties per month (US Government Accountability Office 2009). A Canadian officer characterized the Afghan police as "cannon fodder" in the fight against the Taliban, placed as they were in vulnerable positions without proper training, equipment, or force protection (Wilder 2007). In early 2009, the ANP had an annual attrition rate of 20 percent from combat losses, desertion, disease, and other causes. If that rate were to continue, the equivalent of the entire police force would have to be replaced by 2014, a fact that raises doubts about the possibility of building a competent and stable police organization (US Institute of Peace, Security Sector Reform Working Group 2009).

The Creation of Alternative Security Forces

The ANP's failure to provide security resulted in US efforts to recruit alternative forces to counter the insurgency. In late 2006, the United States authorized the creation of the Afghan National Police Auxiliary (ANPA) in a quick-fix effort to address the renewed Taliban presence in southern Afghanistan. Under this plan, provincial governors could draft a force of 11,271 recruits from 124 high-risk districts in twenty-one provinces into the ANPA. The purpose of the auxiliary force was to man checkpoints and perform community policing functions, thereby freeing the ANP to focus on counterinsurgency operations. Each recruit received five days of classroom instruction on the Afghan constitution, ethics, and police techniques, five days of weapons training, an AK-47 assault rifle, a standard ANP uniform, a US$70 monthly salary, and a one-year contract. By July 2007, some 8,300 ANPA enlistees had received training.

Since they were locally recruited, however, they were vulnerable to factional control and manipulation. Despite initial assertions that they would be thoroughly vetted, many were thought to be Taliban agents and nearly all were members of forces loyal to provincial power brokers. Meanwhile, the creators of the ANPA were widely criticized for reconstituting and legitimizing tribal militias and groups loyal to powerful warlords, thereby reversing the progress made to disband illegally armed groups. The ANPA was also challenged by some ANP officers on the grounds that its recruits received the same salary and wore the same uniform as professional policemen but had far less training and did not owe allegiance to the national government (Wilder 2007, 13–17). But the controversy ended in May 2008 when the ANPA was disbanded as a result of its incompetence and ineffectiveness (Brewster 2008).

Despite the failure of the ANPA, the idea of creating self-defense forces at the village level surfaced again in January 2009 in the form of the Afghanistan Public Protection Program (AP3). Members of this guard force were recruited by tribal *shuras* (councils) to defend their villages against Taliban insurgents. The program began as a pilot project in Wardak Province, a primary gateway into Kabul for insurgents and suicide bombers. Known as Guardians, the first local recruits patrolled roads and communities in districts around the provincial capital of Maidan Shahr. The program was run by the CSTC-A, which provided Kalashnikov rifles and two weeks of training by US Special Forces. The training covered the rule of law, human rights, discipline, and military tactics. The Guardians received the equivalent of US$100 per month, plus US$25 for food, as well as radios and cell phones so they could call for backup from US troops if challenged (Pessin 2008).

The AP3 was part of an integrated and sequenced program to improve security, which also included (1) the deployment of US troops that were part of the surge of forces into Afghanistan; (2) FDD training of locally based ANP units, which were temporarily replaced by ANCOP constabulary; and (3) the provision of development assistance from the Commanders Emergency Response Program (CERP). Districts that cooperated with the program were eligible for an additional US$500,000 in CERP funds. AP3 recruitment began positively in Wardak's northern, ethnic-Tajik districts but met resistance in the southern, ethnic-Pashtun districts, which had kinship ties to the Taliban (Sherman 2009).

The AP3 program was based loosely on the tradition in some parts of Afghanistan of raising village militias known as Arbakai. It also appeared to be modeled on the successful Sons of Iraq program in Iraq, composed of former Sunni insurgents who had turned against Al-Qaida and were funded by the US military (Nelson 2009). Although the initiative reportedly came from the Afghan government, a number of Afghan officials criticized the AP3 for diverting resources and undermining efforts to create a professional national police force. Afghanistan's ambassador to Washington, Said Jawad, told the BBC in January 2009 that since Afghan tribal structures had been weakened by decades of conflict, the plan was risky and could backfire, strengthening only warlords and criminals (Vennard 2009). Members of Parliament warned that arming tribal factions could encourage a civil war. A parliamentarian from Wardak Province noted that the Soviets had created village-level self-defense forces there with disastrous results (Constable 2009).

The Proliferation of Foreign Assistance Programs

The expanded challenges faced by the Afghan police were accompanied by a proliferation in the number of countries participating in the international police assistance program. On June 17, 2007, the European Union Police Mission to Afghanistan (EUPOL) formally replaced Germany as the key partner in police assistance. Initially, EUPOL contained 160 police officers led by a German police general. These highly experienced European officers were supposed to provide much-needed expertise and leadership for the police assistance effort (International Crisis Group 2007). By fall 2007, however, EUPOL was already mired in controversy. The first EUPOL commander resigned after three months as a result of a dispute with the EU's special envoy to Afghanistan; EUPOL also had difficulty in establishing working relations with the NATO-led ISAF and in aligning the varying goals of its member states. In addition, European publics were unenthusiastic about their forces serving in Afghanistan; with many EU member states balking at honoring commitments for personnel, their police were slow to deploy. Although EUPOL's authorized strength was 400 members, it had only 218 police officers on the ground by May 2009 (Sedra 2008).

EUPOL's mission was to monitor, mentor, and advise the Afghans as they established their own civilian law enforcement organization rather than directly train Afghan police personnel. Thus, EUPOL members were located at the MOI in Kabul and in provincial capitals, where they were quartered with Provincial Reconstruction Teams (PRTs). Many EUPOL officers served as members of their national PRTs, although technically they filled personnel slots that were identified as EUPOL. Lack of physical infrastructure and force protection inhibited the expansion of EUPOL into areas where security was not guaranteed. In 2009, the European role in Afghan police assistance was further complicated by the creation of the NATO Training Mission–Afghanistan (NTM-A), which offered the promise of NATO military protection for European police but required that they serve within a military command structure. French Foreign Minister Bernard Kouchner recommended that the European Gendarmerie Force (EGF), a multinational constabulary force with military status, deploy to Afghanistan to provide training. This offered the prospect of another group of European police advisers operating under yet another mandate (US Institute of Peace, Security Sector Reform Working Group 2009).

In addition to the EU, Italy, Canada, the UK, and other coalition partners conducted police assistance programs, assigning teams to their respective PRTs that conducted training and provided equipment and technical assistance. In general, these teams stressed the importance of community policing and taught civilian police skills as a countermeasure to what the Europeans believed was the overly militarized US approach to training. Their programs, which varied in size, reflected a range of national policing philosophies and practices and were not always coordinated with the larger US and EU programs.

European donors claimed that the US efforts to militarize the Afghan police belied its professed intentions to promote democracy and the rule of law. They believed that only with the creation of a professional law enforcement agency capable of controlling crime and securing Afghan society could the Afghan government establish its legitimacy and gain the allegiance of its own people. Generally speaking, the role of the police in successful counterinsurgency efforts is to establish relations with the public, protect citizens against violence, and work as a component of the criminal justice system, along with effective courts and prisons. Only by preparing the ANP to perform this role could the international police assistance program accomplish its objectives of creating a stable, prosperous, and democratic Afghanistan (Legon 2009).

Conclusion

With the benefit of hindsight, it is easy to see what went wrong in Iraq and what continues to go wrong in Afghanistan with respect to local security sector reform:

- Failure to plan for security stabilization after the suppression of organized military resistance
- Underestimation of the personnel and equipment needed to rebuild and train local law enforcement institutions
- Lack of international civilian advisers and trainers
- Poor reputation of local police as auxiliaries to the military
- Insufficient training of local police
- Problems of coordination among coalition members

Having examined how police training under local auspices in Iraq and Afghanistan went awry, we shall now examine how the United States might have avoided these problems based on its own prior experience with postconflict interventions.

2

What We Should Have Learned

The use of police instead of military forces as the primary peacekeepers in postwar conflict areas is an idea whose time has come.

—Graham Day (2001)

Between the end of the Cold War and the conflicts in Iraq and Afghanistan, the United States had a series of experiences with police in postconflict interventions. These interventions were difficult, but each provided lessons that were available to planners of future operations. In all of them, the need to create law and order locally became a major preoccupation as violence and the threat of violence continued postinvasion. In this chapter, we will review these missions to point out the lessons that might have been heeded in Iraq and Afghanistan.

Panama

Operation Iraqi Freedom was remarkably similar to Operation Just Cause, as the US mission in Panama was called. In December 1989, the United States acted unilaterally to remove a threat to its national security by deposing General Manual Noriega, a brutal dictator. Following a quick US military victory, massive looting occurred in Panama City. Neither prepared nor instructed to deal with large-scale civil disorder, US troops stood by as government buildings and the city's commercial district suffered millions of US dollars in damage. The architects of the US plan for postconflict restoration had assumed that a grateful public would welcome US intervention and that Panamanian security forces would maintain public order. Unfortunately, the Panamanian Defense Force (PDF), the country's only security service, had been routed in fighting with US forces and its surviving personnel were in hiding. After five days of rioting, additional US troops and military police were deployed to restore order, but the massive damage to Panama's economy and to public confidence in the new order had already been done. Subsequently, the United States suffered more casualties in combating a stubborn low-level insurgency led by paramilitary "dignity battalions" than it had sustained during major combat operations (Gray and Manwaring 1998).

In the wake of the general breakdown in public order, the Panamanian government recognized that the surviving elements of the PDF could not be demobilized without risking further disorder. Thus, the Panamanian government determined it would enlist vetted PDF personnel to form a new internal security force, the Panamanian National Police (PNP) (Schultz 1993). Responsibility for training this new internal security force was assigned to the US military, but this decision ran afoul of US law. After the United States announced the formal termination of the military phase of operations, Congress adopted the Urgent Assistance to Democracy in Panama Act, which reaffirmed the legal prohibition stipulated in Section 660 of the Foreign Assistance Act against the employment of the US military to train foreign police except in times of war. At the same time, the State Department sought to reduce the Department of Defense's (DOD) involvement with the police-training program on the grounds that it was inconsistent with the US goal of restoring democracy in Panama (Gray and Manwaring 1998). The responsibility for police training was then reassigned to the Department of Justice's (DOJ) International Criminal Investigative Training Assistance Program (ICITAP). ICITAP was created in 1984 to train criminal investigators in Central American countries. Composed of FBI special agents and Spanish-speaking administrative staff, it offered short courses in detective work. ICITAP staffers had never trained an entire police force, so they learned on the job. First they developed a 120-hour transition course in the basic skills needed for policing a democratic society, which was taught to all PNP officers. Over the next two years, ICITAP created two police academies—one for the PNP and the other for the Judicial Technical Police, a detective unit—that trained nearly 3,000 cadets (Perito 2002).

During this period, US military police were permitted to continue joint patrols with the fledging PNP under the guise of so-called liaison and operational activity. The military police acted as mentors, monitoring the PNP performance and reporting back to the academy on shortcomings in the training program. These joint patrols provided essential security while giving the PNP on-the-job training in police operations. Thus they provided a short-term solution to a problem that the United States could not otherwise have addressed. The military police's role was discontinued when the PNP became fully operational (Marenin 1999).

Somalia

On December 3, 1992, the UN Security Council adopted Resolution 794, authorizing a humanitarian relief mission to Somalia (UN Security Council 1992). The core of Operation Restore Hope was a US-led United Task Force (UNITAF) consisting of 38,000 troops (including 28,000 Americans) from more than twenty countries. UNITAF did not include a police mission, but it did become deeply involved in creating an indigenous police force composed of former members of the Somalia National Police (SNP). Before the civil war, the SNP had 15,000 officers and a well-earned reputation for professionalism, fairness, and clan neutrality. During the conflict, the SNP ceased to exist, but its members still avoided taking sides. As UNITAF deployed, former members of the SNP reappeared in their tattered uniforms and voluntarily assisted the troops with traffic control and other police functions. When US Marines began suffering casualties while patrolling the streets of Mogadishu, the US special envoy, Ambassador Robert Oakley, decided that establishing a Somali police force would improve security in Mogadishu and eliminate the need for UNITAF to perform police functions (Perito 2002).

In response to Oakley's recommendation, the DOD authorized UNITAF to help organize the Auxiliary Security Force (ASF). The UNITAF provost marshal and twenty-two US military police provided assistance, but were not allowed by US law to provide training. UNITAF also wrote an ASF handbook complete with administrative and operational guidelines. The former SNP members were assigned variously to traffic control, crowd control, neighborhood patrol, the protection of food distribution sites, and the security of airfields and seaports. Most were unarmed, but UNITAF did provide weapons to those protecting police stations and for use in joint patrols with its own military forces. The ASF performed missions that might have resulted in casualties to the intervention force. Unfortunately, it failed to survive UNITAF's departure and termination of support (Perito 2002).

In May 1993, with relief supplies flowing, famine on the wane, and the country at relative peace, UNITAF withdrew, transferring operations to a significantly less capable UN mission, United Nations Operation in Somalia (UNOSOM) II. Troop strength decreased to 28,000 peacekeepers; only 4,000 US troops remained. The UN Security Council, however, broadened the UNOSOM II mandate to include reestablishing a national government, advancing political reconciliation, disarming Somali factions, and holding Somalis who breached international law accountable. With the US Marines gone, the Somali warlord, General Mohammed Farah Hassan Aideed, immediately challenged the weaker UN military force, ambushing a patrol and killing twenty-four Pakistani peacekeepers. The Security Council condemned the attack and the head of the UN mission in Somalia issued an arrest warrant for Aideed (Perito 2002).

On October 3, 1993, US Army Rangers executed a raid to capture some of Aideed's lieutenants. Two Black Hawk helicopters were shot down, eighteen Army Rangers were killed, eighty-four other US soldiers were wounded, and a US helicopter pilot was captured. Americans were stunned by footage of Somalis dragging the bodies of US soldiers through the streets. In response to a public outcry, President Bill Clinton announced on October 7, 1993, that US military forces would withdraw from Somalia by March 31, 1994, and that the United States would help the UN rebuild the SNP to replace its troops and provide security (Bowden 1999).

Following the president's announcement, the State and Justice Departments began work on a US police assistance program that would do just that. It took six months for the State Department to obtain the presidential waiver required by Section 660 of the Foreign Assistance Act and to convince Congress to permit the use of reprogrammed funds for police training in Somalia. ICITAP trainers arrived in March 1994, established a temporary police academy in the UN compound in Mogadishu, and opened regional training centers in Baidoa and Calcaio. Using US contractors and UN police as instructors, it conducted three twenty-one-day refresher courses for 176 former SNP officers and delivered other courses in weapons handling, convoy escorts, and police station administration. ICITAP then began rebuilding police stations with the help of the UN military. The DOD contributed 353 vehicles, 5,000 M16 rifles, 5,000 pistols, uniforms, and equipment valued at US$25 million. The United States also contributed US$2 million to a UN fund for police salaries (Perito 2002).

But it was too little, too late, as Somalia's warring factions were already proving unable to form a government and instead resumed fighting in Mogadishu. UN convoys were attacked exiting the gates of the UN compound. ICITAP instructors began wearing flak jackets and helmets in the classroom because of the number of stray bullets entering the UN compound from battles in the streets outside. Increasingly unable to function in a war zone, the program was withdrawn in June 1994. Nearly all the US equipment that had been donated by the DOD for the Somalia police was also removed from the country before it could fall into the hands of rival militias (Call 1998). The UN police mission remained until March 1995, when the Security Council terminated UNOSOM II's mandate (UN Secretariat Department of Public Information 1996).

Like Panama, Somalia provided a set of lessons that were instructive for future police training missions in postconflict environments. As we have seen, the Somali police, who had a reputation for professionalism and fairness before the civil conflict, were able to assist the peacekeeping force so long as they were properly equipped, organized, and protected against better-armed militias and criminal gangs. These officers returned to duty voluntarily and worked without pay until funded by the UN. Had Somali political factions been able to achieve political reconciliation, the basis for a future police force was already in place. Instead, their failure to reach a political settlement meant that Somali police had to operate in the absence of a national government under the supervision only of weak local councils. Somalia also showed that indigenous police forces cannot function effectively in the absence of the other two parts of the criminal justice system, namely courts and prisons. Because the UN chose to postpone the revival of the Somali court system until Somalia had a central government (which it did not establish), Somali police were left to take the law into their own hands.

Haiti

Planning for the US-led intervention in Haiti was influenced by what many in the DOD perceived as the failure of the UN peace operation in Somalia. The DOD was determined to prevent the type of mission creep that led to the involvement of US military forces in the effort to capture General Aideed and the Black Hawk Down incident. The DOD was also insistent on having an exit strategy in place that would permit an early US military withdrawal. DOD made clear that US military forces would not perform police functions and that an effective indigenous security force would have to be created to maintain public order. The goal was to recruit and train a Haitian police force that could provide internal security and permit the quick departure of US forces. The problem was that Haiti had never had such a force (Kozak 2000).

Indeed, the only security force on the island was the Haitian Army, known as the Forces Armees d'Haiti, which performed both military and police functions. In a September 1991 coup, the army had overthrown Haiti's first democratically elected president, Jean Bertrand Aristide, and established a military dictatorship. It was an untrained and ill-equipped force of 7,000 men supported by uncounted numbers of thugs called Attaches. Many soldiers were guilty of gross human rights abuses, murder, torture, and other criminal activities. During the planning for the Haiti mission, it appeared the Haitian Army would resist US intervention (Bailey, Maguire, and Pouliot 1998). The question was how to dismantle the army only to recruit some of its members for an interim security force that would serve while a new civilian police force was being trained.

The answer was the creation of a force of 920 International Police Monitors (IPMs) from twenty-six countries primarily in Europe, the Middle East, and Latin America. Under the 1993 Governors Island Accord signed by Haitian strongman General Cedras and President Aristide, the IPMs carried sidearms, had arrest powers, and could use deadly force in self-defense or to prevent Haitian-on-Haitian violence. The IPMs' initial mission was to supervise an Interim Public Security Force (IPSF) of 3,000 former members of the Haitian army. After being vetted for crimes and human rights offenses, IPSF members received a one-week orientation course in democratic policing. They were given new uniforms and sent back into the streets under the watchful eye of the IPMs. This interim force was subsequently reduced in stages that coincided with the deployment of a new, US-trained indigenous police force, the Haitian National Police (HNP) (Neild 1995).

Applying lessons learned from previous operations, the IPM commissioner, former New York City Police Department Commissioner Ray Kelly, reported directly to the commanding officer of the Multinational Force (MNF) as part of a unified chain of command. IPM national contingents were assigned as units to geographic sectors or specific functional responsibilities. For example, an elite Israeli police unit was given responsibility for the poorest and most dangerous slum in Port au Prince. IPMs were located in Haitian police stations along with US military police. Patrols were conducted by "four men in a Jeep," a concept borrowed from the earlier experience in Panama. This concept brought together a military police driver, an IPM officer, an IPSF officer, and an interpreter who rode together in one MNF vehicle so that all police elements with full collective powers were present. The vehicle was usually followed or monitored by a military patrol in case backup was needed (Kelly 1995).

Following the MNF's arrival in Haiti, representatives of ICITAP began working with their French and Canadian counterparts to establish Haiti's first national police academy. At its peak, the joint program employed more than 300 trainers and interpreters to train some 3,000 cadets. When the Haitian government increased the number of requested HNP officers from 3,500 to 5,000, a second campus was opened at Fort Leonard Wood, Missouri. By February 1996, some 5,243 new Haitian police officers had completed training. As new recruits graduated from the academy, they were placed under the supervision of IPM monitors, who acted as their field training officers. Once they deployed, corresponding units of the IPSF were demobilized and assigned to job training programs or returned to private life (Perito 1998). In the view of most observers, Operation Uphold Democracy successfully achieved its objectives, which included removing the Cedras regime, restoring President Aristide to power, and handing off responsibility to the UN Mission in Haiti in six months.

The success of the Haiti operation demonstrated that lessons could be applied from earlier missions and that a US-led intervention could achieve its objectives and hand over its responsibilities to a UN mission. The Haiti operation also proved that US military police, international police, and local police could be co-located and could conduct joint patrols with military support. The four-men-in-a-Jeep approach helped to quickly restore and maintain public order while providing effective supervision of indigenous police personnel. The joint patrols were made possible by the creation of a unified chain of command for military and police forces and the co-location of the MNF and IPM headquarters. Shared communications and integrated planning maximized collaboration and increased the effectiveness of both the military and police.

In addition, Haiti showed that international police could be armed and given executive authority to make arrests and perform other police functions. In previous peace operations, by comparison, UN police were unarmed and could only monitor the local police and report untoward behavior. The fact that the international police were armed made them less vulnerable and more confident, hence more assertive in controlling potentially violent situations. Unfortunately, the authority for the police to carry arms rested on the Governors Island Accord and was not seen by the UN as a precedent for future operations (Bailey, Maguire, and Pouliot 1998).

Bosnia and Herzegovina

After three weeks of negotiations at Wright Patterson Air Force Base in Dayton, Ohio, the Bosnian war ended on November 21, 1995, with the initialing of the General Framework Agreement for Peace in Bosnia and Herzegovina. Issues relating to the role of the police were contained in Annex 11, titled "International Police Task Force." The Dayton Accords provided that the Bosnian entities would be responsible for creating a safe and secure environment for all persons in their jurisdictions by maintaining civilian law enforcement agencies, which would operate in accordance with respect for human rights and fundamental freedoms. The parties to the agreement requested that the UN Security Council establish a UN International Police Task Force (IPTF) to assist Bosnian law enforcement agencies in this effort (Office of the High Representative and EU Special Representative 1995).

The mandate and organization of the IPTF was the result of an agreement between US and European diplomats and not the product of negotiations with the parties to the peace agreement. It also was not the work of police experts, as there were none at Dayton, according to a State Department legal adviser we interviewed. European negotiators wanted an unarmed IPTF with a weak mandate, as did the DOD (International Crisis Group 2002). The US military wanted to ensure that the NATO-led Implementation Force (IFOR) was the only legitimate armed force in Bosnia. It was afraid that an armed IPTF with an aggressive mandate might get into trouble and that the IFOR would be forced to perform police functions. The US military argued that this would constitute "mission creep," another imprecise mission like Somalia that would lead to greater endangerment of US forces (Holbrooke 1999).

Under the Dayton Accords, the IPTF would be unarmed and would rely on the local police and the IFOR for protection. It was envisioned solely as an international civilian police force that would monitor, advise, and train Bosnian police, who would be responsible for law enforcement and citizen protection. Should its advice be ignored, the IPTF's only recourse, according to Annex 11, Article V, was to notify either the Office of the High Representative (OHR)—which was established under the Dayton Accords to oversee the peace process—or the IFOR commander, who could then bring the breach in conduct to the attention of the UN, the Joint Civilian Commission, or the relevant parties. Given its lack of authority, the IPTF needed the cooperation of Bosnian law enforcement authorities to achieve the Dayton Accords' objectives of restoring law and public order, freedom of movement, and justice as the basis for a lasting peace (Gow 1997).

The prospects for such cooperation were, however, doubtful. What the drafters at Dayton failed to appreciate was that the nature of the Bosnian conflict meant that the police forces of the three rival parties were ethnically based. This meant that they were unlikely to provide protection or police services to minorities. Since the IPTF was unarmed and had no police powers, there would be no police force in Bosnia to protect minorities, nor any means beyond persuasion for the IPTF to compel compliance with the Dayton Accords. While the IFOR could provide area security and reinforce patrols to deter lawlessness, its forces would not be trained or equipped to control demonstrations or perform routine law enforcement functions. Furthermore, the appeals to the High Representative would be of limited utility, as that office had little authority and few resources.

On December 21, 1995, the Security Council adopted resolution 1035, which created the UN Mission in Bosnia and Herzegovina (UNMBIH) and established the IPTF with an authorized strength of 1,721 international police monitors, several hundred of whom were Americans. The US contingent was provided by DynCorp International under contract with the State Department. Some forty-three countries provided personnel, but the IPTF was extremely slow to deploy, and only a few hundred police were present when the task force faced its first test early in 1996. Under Dayton, control of the Sarajevo suburbs, which are located on high ground surrounding the city, was transferred from the Serb military to the Bosniak-Croat Federation to make the city less vulnerable to attacks by artillery should the war resume. Over 100,000 ethnic Serbs inhabited these areas. Many were longtime residents. As the deadline for the transfer approached, hard-line Serb leaders in the town of Pale ordered Serb residents to evacuate and to destroy everything they could not carry. Departing Serbs were ordered to thoroughly loot, burn, and destroy buildings so that incoming Federation authorities would find a wasteland.

The OHR allowed ethnic Serb police to remain in the suburban municipalities on the assumption they would protect Serb residents. Instead, accompanied by groups of Serb thugs, they engaged in what amounted to ethnic self-cleansing, forcing as many as 30,000 Serb residents that might have stayed to withdraw. From late February to mid-March, all Serb residents were either evacuated or were forced to leave for the Republika Srpska—taking the wiring, windows, and pipes from their apartments and destroying or booby trapping what could not be removed. Some families even exhumed and carried off the bodies of their relatives (Wentz 1998). Television footage of burning buildings and fleeing refugees gave the world an image of general lawlessness that the international intervention force was unable to control.

During the evacuation, the IFOR, though present in force, did nothing to stop it. As the destruction proceeded, its troops stood by and watched, refusing requests for protection from Bosnian civilians. Though the IFOR had the capacity to prevent the destruction of property and the violent expulsion of thousands of residents, Admiral Leighton Smith, the first US commander of IFOR, considered police functions outside of its mandate. One IFOR spokesman stated that although the arson was "unfortunate," the Serbs had the right to burn their own houses; another put it more bluntly: "IFOR is not a police force and will not undertake police functions" (Holbrooke 1998). Its failure to prevent the violence was a defining moment for the international presence, setting a bleak tone for the initial phase of the peace operation.

In the wake of the transfer of the Sarajevo suburbs, the IPTF's primary task was to downsize the various Bosnian police forces, which had ballooned to nearly 70,000 personnel with the addition of former soldiers at the end of the war. The goal was to remove all those without police experience and to create a force with an officer-to-population ratio consistent with European standards (Wasserman 1996)—but it was complicated by the Dayton Accords' confirmation of the wartime division of Bosnia into the Bosniak-Croat Federation and Republika Srpska. The Federation's internal security was the responsibility of a small Federation police force and independent forces in each of its ten cantons. In the Republika Srpska, there was a single, entirely separate police force under the tight central control of ethnic-Serb authorities. At first, these various forces cooperated poorly with the IPTF—when they cooperated at all. Matters began to improve, however, in April 1996, when the IPTF convened an international conference on police restructuring in Petersburg, a suburb of Bonn, Germany. Federation officials, UN representatives, and senior IPTF officers attended the meeting along with delegations from donor countries, including the United States. Officials and police from the Republika Srpska were invited but did not attend (Wentz 1998).

The resulting Petersburg Declaration, signed on April 25, 1996, provided for a two-thirds reduction in the size of the Federation police forces to 11,500 (Office of the High Representative and EU Special Representative 1996). Restructuring was to be accomplished through a screening process that would remove imposters, criminals, and human rights offenders and apply standards established by the IPTF, namely graduation from a police academy and a good professional record. Applicants' names were checked against the database of the International Criminal Tribunal for the Former Yugoslavia in The Hague. They were also published in local newspapers with an invitation for persons with negative information to come forward. Candidates who survived the vetting process would then take a written examination as well as physical and psychological tests. They would also have to undergo a two-part transition-training program conducted by the IPTF. Any police officer not certified by this process would be dismissed from the force. Any armed person who was not a certified police officer would be dealt with by the IFOR (Office of the High Representative and EU Special Representative 1996). Officials in the Republika Srpska initially refused to accept the IPTF certification and training plan; thus police assistance was provided only to the Federation until 1997, when the Republika Srpska finally signed a similar cooperation agreement.

During the first year of the Bosnian mission, ICITAP supported the IPTF as it deployed across the country. Initially, ICITAP provided its officers with training in human rights, monitoring, and reporting violations. It also developed the two courses that were required for all Bosnian police officers as part of the certification process—a forty-hour course in human dignity and a 120-hour course in basic police skills—and prepared IPTF and local police instructors to teach them. The shorter course, which used an interactive discussion format, provided its students with an understanding of the importance of protecting the human rights and preserving the personal dignity of all people, regardless of ethnic origin. The longer course covered the fundamentals of patrols, traffic control, criminal investigations, arrest procedures, interviewing witnesses, report writing, first aid, and the role of police in a democratic society. By early 2000, all 20,000 officers in the Republika and the Federation were scheduled to receive both courses.

In 1998, ICITAP had also begun working with the IPTF to develop a curriculum for the recently reopened police academies in Sarajevo and in the Republika Srpska. It conducted training programs in academy management, curriculum design, and classroom instruction for Bosnian academy executives and staff. It also developed a field training program for academy graduates that was staffed by IPTF personnel. That same year, the two organizations cocreated an emergency management system, emergency command centers, and the Public Order Major Incident Management Unit. They developed policies and procedures for emergency response, provided equipment and training, and ran practical disaster exercises to test the readiness of the system and its personnel. By 1999, then, the US and UN police assistance programs together had not only established two police academies that were training both cadets and officers and established a fully functioning emergency response system but also nearly completed the certification process for all police officers in the country (Perito 1998).

Kosovo

Unlike Bosnia, Kosovo had no local police. During the conflict, Yugoslav Interior Ministry Special Police Units (MUPs) were responsible for some of the worst incidents of ethnic cleansing. Under the terms of the Military Technical Agreement (MTA) signed June 10, 1999, between NATO and the Federal Republic of Yugoslavia, Yugoslav security forces, including the civilian police, were withdrawn from Kosovo. The resulting vacuum was filled by a US-led force of 45,000 NATO and coalition troops, including 7,000 US soldiers, and the UN Mission in Kosovo (UNMIK) police force of 7,000, including more than 800 US officers (Dobbins et al. 2003). Police had full authority, including the right to make arrests, detain suspects, and use deadly force. Security Council Resolution 1244 stipulated that the principal responsibilities of the "international civil presence" would include "maintaining civil law and order, including establishing local police forces and meanwhile [*sic*] through the deployment of international police personnel to Kosovo" (UN Security Council 1999). This was the first time the UN had embarked on an armed executive police mission in a region where there was no host government. In addition, UNMIK was responsible for supervising the establishment of a new, multiethnic Kosovo Police Service (KPS). This meant the UN was faced with the challenge of creating and maintaining two police forces at the same time (International Crisis Group 2000).

Per the internationally agreed upon division of labor in Kosovo, training for the KPS was provided by the Organization for Security and Cooperation in Europe (OSCE). This involved establishing the Kosovo Police Service School (KPSS) and training a cadre of police officers who proportionally represented all ethnic groups, including Serbs. The KPSS was located in the town of Vucitrn, twenty-five kilometers north of the capital of Pristina on the fully remodeled campus of a former MUP training center. The school opened on September 7, 1999, with an initial class of 200 multiethnic students selected from more than 19,500 applicants. Once it was fully operational in March 2000, the KPSS was staffed by 200 international police instructors from twenty-two OSCE member-states with a complement of 600 cadets in training at any time. The directorship, one-quarter of the school's training staff, and the basic curriculum were all provided by ICITAP. The newly renovated facility had the capacity to house up to 705 students, with separate quarters for men and women. It also had two gyms, a weight room, a mess hall, a laundry, a warehouse, an armory, medical and administrative offices, and twenty-eight classrooms. During the first years of UNMIK, the KPSS was the only multiethnic institution functioning in Kosovo (Organization for Security and Cooperation in Europe 2005).

The OSCE's mandate was to provide "democratically oriented police training" for 5,300 KPS officers by December 21, 2002. At the KPSS, students underwent twelve weeks of basic police instruction under the guidance of international OSCE police instructors. Lessons were delivered in English and translated by local assistants into both Serbian and Albanian. Courses covered patrol duties, the use of force, basic criminal investigation, forensics, traffic control, defensive tactics, first aid, applicable laws, interviewing techniques, and report writing. Following graduation, officers were assigned to fifteen weeks of structured field training under the supervision of UNMIK Police and KPS field training officers, who were also trained by the international staff of the KPSS. Trainees spent nine weeks of the total in the field and six weeks at the KPSS or a regional training center for additional time in the classroom. After completing a total of twenty-seven weeks of classroom and field instruction, the new KPS officers were eligible for certification and independent assignment. In addition to basic training, the KPSS offered what it called a First Line Supervisors Course for senior police managers as well as advanced courses in a number of specialized police skills such as criminal and accident investigations. The school also offered a trainer certification program for KPS instructors, who increasingly assumed responsibility for teaching at the school (Organization for Security and Cooperation in Europe 2005).

To ensure that the KPS remained the multiethnic, community-oriented force that it was shaping up to be—one that could eventually replace the UNMIK police—recruiting quotas were established for women (20 percent) and minorities, including Serbs (15 percent). The UN agreed that half of the original cadre of 4,000 officers would be former members of the Kosovo Liberation Army. To ensure a measure of experience, the UN also determined that 25 percent would be drawn from the ranks of those who had served as police officers in Kosovo during the period of provincial autonomy that ended in 1989. Unfortunately, this left little opportunity for unaffiliated, ethnic Albanian men who were otherwise qualified. Recruits were required to be between twenty-one and fifty-five years old, to be in good health, and to have a secondary education and a strong moral character. They also had to pass a UN-administered oral interview, a written exam, and psychological, medical, and physical tests. Furthermore, they were required to undergo a background investigation; if a record of human rights abuses or criminal activities turned up, they were disqualified. The screening process had an 80 percent failure rate, primarily based on educational deficiencies and poor scores on the written examination (Kovchok 2001).

The KPS operated under the watchful eyes of the UNMIK Police Planning and Development Department. After graduating from the KPSS and completing field training, KPS officers were assigned to UNMIK police stations (ethnic Serbs served only in communities with Serbian majorities), where they functioned as auxiliaries, because the UN was unwilling to create a separate institution until a decision on Kosovo's final status had been made. In its first months on the job, the KPS made a positive impression. Despite problems of low pay (380 DM per month), ill-fitting Norwegian uniforms, and inadequate vehicles and equipment, KPS members took their responsibilities seriously. They initially worked unarmed, as it took the UN four months to provide them with sidearms; on several occasions, officers came face-to-face with armed criminals. Fortunately, there were no casualties. Officers also had to deal with the public distrust of the police that lingered from the days of Communist rule. Finally, they were hampered by inadequate judicial and penal systems, which took much longer to begin functioning (Kovchok 2001).

Within two years, however, the KPS had assumed responsibility for providing basic police services. By July 2002, there were more KPS officers than there were UNMIK police. Some 4,770 officers had completed training and entered active service, compared to 4,524 internationals in the UN police force. KPS officers comprised between 65 and 75 percent of the police serving in four of five regions and had taken over responsibility for most routine operations. The exception to the general takeover of routine duties by local officers was the city of Mitrovica, a flash point for repeated clashes between ethnic Albanians and Serbs, and the Serb-dominated area to the north where only a few ethnic-Serb KPS officers were deployed.

With the shift in balance between UN and Kosovo police, UNMIK began implementing a plan for the orderly transition of responsibility for law enforcement to the KPS. A senior rank structure for the KPS was introduced, and 203 sergeants and twenty lieutenants were appointed. At the end of 2002, UNMIK transferred full responsibility for patrol duties to the KPS, with the UN police acting as monitors. At about the same time it transferred responsibility for one of the five regional police headquarters. Over the next two years, the KPS staff would grow to 6,300, gradually assuming responsibility for more functions and the management of more regional centers. By 2006, police leadership, management, and operation, as well as "the keys to the main police headquarters," would be in the hands of the KPS (Kovchok 2001).

In his predeparture press conference on December 17, 2000, Bernard Kouchner, the first Special Representative of the Secretary-General to head UNMIK, said that the lesson of Kosovo was that "peacekeeping missions need to arrive with a law-and-order kit made up of trained police, judges, and prosecutors and a set of draconian security laws. This is the only way to stop criminal behavior from flourishing in a postwar vacuum of authority" (J. R. Smith 2000). Indeed, throughout the first two years of the Kosovo mission, the slow arrival of UN police contingents and the unwillingness of the KFOR to deal with civil disorder allowed for continued high levels of politically motivated violence, illicit trafficking, and street crime. The UN's inability to rapidly restore order and establish the rule of law undermined the international mission and encouraged extremists to engage in ethnic violence. It was not until 2001 when nearly 4,400 UN police officers, including nine of ten constabulary units, were in place did the violence subside (Perito 2004). The lesson of Kosovo was that the UN had to establish police, courts, and prisons at the beginning of its mission in order to restore order and create the conditions for economic development and political reconciliation.

Conclusion

The US police assistance program in Kosovo marked the end of a learning process for the United States, one that began in Panama with the creation of indigenous police forces in peacekeeping operations. Looking back, we see that several lessons might have been learned.

1. In postintervention environments, local police are normally unprepared, unwilling, or unfit to provide police services. As a result, looting, civil disorder, and crime increase until and unless the intervention forces in question take action.
2. The failure of intervention forces to provide a safe and secure environment leads to a loss of popular support and endangers the success of the mission.
3. US military forces are neither trained nor equipped to control civil disorder. Furthermore, they believe that police duties should not be undertaken by military professionals. UN- and NATO-led military forces have likewise proven untrained, ill-equipped, and extremely reluctant to deal with looting and large-scale civil disorder by unarmed civilians. Properly trained and equipped civilian police can prevent the destruction that results from such unrest, which almost inevitably occurs during the initial phase of these interventions. It is important, therefore, that intervention forces include a police component capable of restoring public order and establishing the rule of law. This force should include both constabulary units that are able to deal with threats to public order and civilian units that can enforce the law, control traffic, and provide standard police service while ensuring that unarmed looters and other types of lawbreakers are dealt with by nonlethal means, arrested, and incarcerated.
4. The presence of international civilian police in intervention forces encourages local police to return to duty under proper supervision in the shortest time. It also promotes the rapid redevelopment of local police institutions, including new training programs.
5. The international police mission should arrive with a detailed plan for either reforming the indigenous police force to ensure that it respects human rights and operates in accordance with democratic principles or creating an entirely new force to replace the old one.

6. The local police force should not be viewed as auxiliary or paramilitary. It should be viewed as a civil force accountable to the rule of law.

7. Military police and foreign police with executive authority should not be asked to train local police. That task should be assigned to experienced police academy personnel who can mange educational institutions, develop curricula, and apply the techniques of adult education.

8. Developing an effective police organization and training an efficient police service is expensive and resource intensive, and it takes at least five years even under optimal conditions. Attempts to rush training in order to put boots on the ground inevitably fails to meet either the short-term need for security or the long-term requirement for establishing the rule of law. Police training cannot be part of an exit strategy. It requires an extended international presence to ensure that lessons taught in the classroom become part of the police culture, replacing attitudes and procedures from the preintervention period.

9. Developing, reforming, and reconstructing the security sector, including the police, takes political commitment on the part of the newly created government. It means making choices and allocating resources. Because policing is a fundamental part of governance, it is inherently political, and government leaders must have the fortitude to stand up to vested interests, partisans, and criminal spoilers who want to prolong the conflict for their own purposes.

10. Finally, intervention forces must be prepared to use diplomatic pressure to ensure that their efforts to create local police that are effective and accountable to the rule of law succeed. The provision of training and material resources is not sufficient in itself.

3

The Role of the Police in Controlling Violence

The lesson to be learnt is that even if an armed insurgency is defeated, the political and subversive struggle will go on and can still win.
—Robert Thompson (1966, 47)

There is a remarkable consensus among experts about what governments must do in order to effectively control violence. This consensus, expressed in the following three principles, represents a convergence of learning across three categories of violence control, namely, insurgency, terrorism, and criminality:

1. Capturing, killing, or imprisoning people who commit violent acts does not mitigate insecurity in the long term unless the identification of perpetrators or targets is guided by precise intelligence.
2. The great effectiveness multiplier in the use of state power against violence is the allegiance and support of the public.
3. In order for governments to gain public support, the responsibility for security should be entrusted as much as possible to police deployed among the population who minimize the use of force and who act in accordance with human rights standards.

This chapter will examine the emergence of these principles as generally accepted doctrine in counterinsurgency, counterterrorism, and crime control and consider the reasoning behind them.

Counterinsurgency

The essential insight of contemporary counterinsurgency (COIN) doctrine is that an insurgency is not simply a fight among armed combatants, rebels, and military but a political struggle for the allegiance of a population (US Army/US Marine Corps 2007). Insurgency is politics conducted with violence. The key requirement for a government is therefore to discredit the insurgents while simultaneously developing popular support for itself. To quote the assessment of a US government interagency task force, "The purpose of COIN is to secure the support of the population for and recapture the monopoly of force by the legitimate government" (US Department of State 2007, 5).

The key tactic for achieving this objective is protecting the public from insurgent violence in a way that minimizes harm. Commanders should thus "transition security activities from combat operations to law enforcement as quickly as possible" (US Army/US Marine Corps 2007). This transition is fundamental to implementing governmental reform and economic development. The implications for military operations are as follows:

- Legitimacy of the local government is the main objective, based on its becoming effective.
- Because political factors are primary, political and diplomatic personnel must be involved in all decisions, even military ones.
- Commanders must understand the human environment of operations, including key groups, tensions and relations, ideologies, values, interests, motivations, means of communication, and leadership systems.
- Intelligence drives operations.
- Support for insurgents should be undermined by separating them in the public mind from their cause. This change in attitude is more important than killing them.
- The security of the population under the rule of law is essential (US Army/US Marine Corps 2007).

The COIN consensus requires what has been called a population-centered as opposed to an insurgent-centered approach, whereby practitioners must act in new and sometimes paradoxical ways:

- Sometimes, the more you protect yourself, the less secure you may be.
- Sometimes, the more force is used, the less effective it is.
- The more successful the counterinsurgency is, the less force can be used and the more risk must be accepted.

- Sometimes doing nothing is the best action.
- Some of the best weapons for counterinsurgents do not shoot.
- The host nation doing something tolerable is normally better than us doing it well.
- If a tactic works this week, it might not work next week; if it works in this province, it might not work in the next.
- Tactical success guarantees nothing.
- Many important decisions are not made by generals (US Army/US Marine Corps 2007; see also Petraeus 2006).

If security in COIN is to be transferred as quickly as possible from the military to civil authorities, then the police become critical. Their primary role, however, is not to augment the offensive capability of the military but to defeat the insurgency in its political dimension (Thompson 1966; US Army/US Marine Corps 2007). There is an explicit division of labor between the police and the military. The military conducts offensive operations designed to capture and kill insurgents, guided by accurate intelligence that minimizes collateral damage to the general population; it also provides a defensive cordon around areas largely cleared of insurgent violence. Within that cordon, the police establish stations that provide "essential police services and have the police recognized as friends, not enemies, of the average citizen" (Corum 2006). Their fighting capacity is limited to reactive defense of the perimeter. In other words, the police role is defensive and centered on the needs of particular populations (Rosenau 2007; Tomes 2004; US Department of State 2007).

Given the responsibility for fighting subversion within the cordon, police may create stability units to deal with challenges that are beyond the capacity of general duties police. These constabulary units, modeled on the French gendarmerie and Italian carabinieri, receive both military and police training and are equipped with armored vehicles and automatic weapons. Their primary purpose is crowd control, especially during demonstrations, strikes, and riots.

Within the bubble of military security, police are expected to treat insurgents as criminals rather than targets beyond the protection of law. They arrest suspects on evidence and submit them to legally authorized judicial proceedings (Thompson 1966; US Army/US Marine Corps 2007). In order for them to win the allegiance of the people, their power must be carefully regulated by law within a justice system that respects human rights (US Army/US Marine Corps 2007; Thompson

1966; Corum 2006). An important objective of this division of labor with the military is to improve operational intelligence about insurgent supporters, networks, and plans. Much of this may come through the daily interaction of police with the population—which doesn't, however, preclude the creation of a covert police intelligence capability as well (Corum 2006; US Department of State 2007; Thompson 1966; Tomes 2004). In short, if the essence of COIN is to clear, hold, and build, then the role of the police is to act as support to the military during the clearing phrase, become a full-fledged partner with the military according to an understood division of labor during the holding phase, and take over as lead agents in the building phase.

Saying that the police must gain the allegiance and support of the people doesn't mean that they don't use force, punishment, and repression (Petraeus 2006; US Army/US Marine Corps 2007). COIN operations may involve regulating the transportation of food, enforcing mandatory curfews, and restricting suspects' movements (Ellison and Smyth 2000; Kitson 1971; Thompson 1966). What is essential, however, is that such powers, however hard edged, be used transparently within a rule of law, so that the populace knows what the rules are and can observe the fairness of their application. This means the police actions should not be governed by martial law—that is, by general rather than specific grants of authority—and should be available to adjudication in open courts rather than in camera or in military tribunals (Kitson 1971; Thompson 1966).

In some successful COIN operations, such as occurred in Malaya during the 1950s, mobile light infantry units were created within the police that carried the fight into the jungle sanctuaries of the insurgents in order to keep them off balance and on the defensive (Kahl 2007; Kitson 1971; Nagl 2002; Thompson 1966). Specially trained and equipped border police may also be developed to monitor the open spaces between checkpoints and to interdict insurgent movement across international borders.

The essential lesson of COIN, however, is that any use of force—military or police—must serve a political purpose, namely delegitimating the insurgents and legitimating the government. Successful COIN is a matter of balancing the kinds of force used, not foregoing force altogether. Getting the balance right between "hard" and "soft" uses of force is the key strategic decision.

The consensus about COIN that we have outlined is drawn primarily from US sources (US Department of State 2007; US Army/US Marine Corps 2007). It is part of an outpouring of writings by military scholars and practitioners since the invasions of Iraq and Afghanistan (Bulloch 1996; Corum 2006; Kahl 2007; Kilcullen 2006; Nagl 2002). These writings draw heavily on an older body of works from around the world about counterinsurgency, notably the operations of the French in Vietnam and Algeria during the 1950s, the British in Malaya and Kenya in the 1950s, and the United States in Vietnam. Indeed, there is hardly anything in the *US Army/US Marine Corps Counterinsurgency Field Manual* (2007) that wasn't discussed by Sir Robert Thompson in his analyses of the shortcomings of US operations in Vietnam forty years ago (1966). As Bruce Hoffman says, Iraq prompted "the seemingly continuous process of rediscovery and reinvention of the counterinsurgency wheel" (Hoffman 2004, 7). The point is that although the sources reported here are mostly from the United States, the consensus about COIN is international and applies to multilateral as well as bilateral counterinsurgency operations.

The importance of the police in counterinsurgency operations has also been supported by several historical analyses. The most extensive study of COIN is by John Ellis, written in 1995, well before the Iraq War. Analyzing 160 "guerrilla wars," to use his term, from that of the Scythians in 156 B.C. to that of the Soviets in Afghanistan (1978–1993), he concluded that support from the people was essential to success (Ellis 1995). This, of course, is the fundamental premise of the contemporary COIN consensus. A US Department of Defense (DOD) study group (2006) analyzed thirty-four counterinsurgencies from 1948 onward and found that in all the cases in which COIN was successful, the police had gained the public's trust, whereas in all the unsuccessful cases, the police had neither participated significantly nor made effective contact with the population. In another study, Kaliv Sepp found that in seventeen twentieth-century insurgencies for which there was reliable information about police activity, the latter's success depended on (1) the police taking the lead role with the military's support; (2) the expansion and diversification of the police; (3) the separation of the insurgents from the general population; and (4) a strategic focus on the basic needs of the population, including safety (2005). Failure, on the other hand, correlated with the primacy of military operations, priority given to kill or capture as opposed to engaging the population, and wide open borders.

Although there is agreement about the general principles of counterinsurgency operations, there are gaps in its operational directions for the police. In particular, it fails to stipulate when police can effectively be deployed to carry out their COIN function. This is a complicated determination, involving assessments of insecurity as well as of the physical and social environment in question. This will be discussed in Chapter 4. The other gap in COIN doctrine from the point of view of police concerns training guidelines. This will be examined in Chapter 5.

Counterterrorism

Police can prevent and control terrorism in three ways, all heavily dependent on the cooperation of the public: (1) by protecting vulnerable people and places on the basis of assessments of the likelihood of attack (target hardening); (2) by investigating, arresting, and prosecuting terrorist suspects, thus providing deterrence against future attacks; and (3) by taking preemptive action designed to stop attacks before they occur on the basis of intelligence about terrorist perpetrators or targets (Bayley and Weisburd 2009; Chapman et al. 2002). What kinds of police are needed to perform each of these tasks?

Target Hardening

The protection of people and places will be done largely by uniformed general duties police and formed police units (FPUs) (Clarke and Newman 2006; Howard 2004). Their protective ability may be increased substantially if the public itself takes protective action, such as being alert to suspicious activity, monitoring access to premises, and installing surveillance equipment (Lyons 2002; O'Hanlon 2005). Playing a critical role in target hardening are private security companies, whose personnel now outnumber the public police in many countries (Bayley and Shearing 2001; Howard 2004; Nelson A. Rockefeller Institute of Government 2003). Police need to be able to work cooperatively with the private sector, coordinating activities and sharing information. Obviously, defensive prevention is more likely to be successful if it is guided by intelligence about terrorist plans. Responsibility for providing this will be discussed later in this chapter.

Criminal Investigation

In countries where terrorism is treated as crime rather than military combat, the police will be responsible for the investigation of terrorist incidents. Investigations will be handled primarily by detectives—specialist nonuniformed members of the police. The British, for example, decided in the early 1970s not to treat IRA terrorists as political prisoners, let alone enemy combatants, but as criminals (Ellison and Smyth 2000). This accomplished two purposes: it contributed to the delegitimation of IRA activities and put the prosecution of terrorist suspects under explicit rules of criminal law adjudicated in open courts, thus making counterterrorism investigations available in principle for public inspection. We say "in principle" because countries under threat from terrorists may pass laws considerably truncating normal trial procedures. The so-called Diplock courts in Northern Ireland, for instance, allowed for single-judge, nonjuried trials in which evidence obtained through coerced confessions and the testimony of informers could be admitted (Aolain 2000; Ellison and Smyth 2000; Holland and Phoenix 1996). Israel, too, currently requires terrorist arrests and prosecutions within its borders as delineated in 1967 to be conducted by the police. In the West Bank and Gaza Strip, on the other hand, terrorists are subject to the rules of war and military justice. Requiring the police to act according to the law doesn't guarantee fairness, but it does ensure transparency.

The key to the successful prosecution of terrorist suspects is reliable testimony from perpetrators, accomplices, and witnesses. Studies have shown that investigations of ordinary reported crimes will be successful only 10 percent of the time unless the suspect has been identified in some reliable way—be it by name, family relationship, place of residence, automobile license, or other method (Bayley 1997; Eck 1982; Greenwood, Petersilia, and Chaikken 1977). In other words, information provided by the public is the starting point of successful criminal investigations. There is no reason to think the situation is any different for investigations of terrorism.

There is one important qualification to this statement. The prosecution of terrorist suspects becomes immeasurably easier and less dependent on public assistance when police are allowed to submit evidence collected by covert means. This is generally not allowed in democratic countries, however, because it compromises the openness and accountability of the criminal justice system. The principle is that extraordinary powers such as covert interdiction should only be used to prevent extraordinary harm, not to prosecute run-of-the-mill crime. Compromising the openness of police prosecution might also damage the reputation of the police for fairness, thereby undermining the public's willingness to engage with them. The most common way of preventing covert operations from contaminating investigations and prosecutions is to create a "wall" between intelligence operatives and criminal investigators, so that information gathered under special authorizations cannot be given to detectives investigating ordinary crimes. Information can flow in reverse, however, from criminal investigators to intelligence specialists. In this way, the secrecy required for clandestine intelligence gathering cannot undercut the transparency of normal police operations. It is important, however, to ensure that intelligence gathered under special authorizations can be passed along to law enforcement agencies as a means to prevent terrorist attacks. Mechanisms can be created to protect the sources and methods of intelligence collection even as general duties police are alerted to the likelihood of attack.

Preemptive Disruption

Target hardening and criminal prosecution are the responsibilities of police everywhere. These activities must be conducted openly (although not necessarily by personnel in uniform), regulated by law, and subject in principle to public review. They involve close interaction between the police and the public, whose willingness to assist determines their success. This is not true of the third form of police counterterrorism activity, namely the preemptive disruption of terrorist plans.

Faced with terrorists willing to engage in widespread killing and even use weapons of mass destruction, governments will be reluctant to rely on passive defense or deterrent punishment. They generally want to accumulate information about attacks and stop them before they occur. What should the role of the police be in this and is the participation of the public important to it?

In a survey of covert counterterrorism in twelve democratic countries, Bayley and Weisburd (2009) found the following:

- Most countries have specialized agencies separate from the police that engage in counterterrorism operations abroad.
- All countries have agencies that specialize in the collection of domestic intelligence about potentially violent subversion but that may or may not have powers of arrest and prosecution. For example, the FBI in the United States does; the UK's MI5 does not.

- All police services, whether centralized or decentralized, engage in domestic counterterrorism as part of their core responsibilities.
- There are no examples of specialized counterterrorism agencies separate from the police at subnational levels.

Although all police engage in covert counterterrorism, there is general agreement among police executives and terrorism experts that covert counterterrorism operations cannot be relied on exclusively to prevent terrorism. Successful counterterrorism requires the active assistance of publicly identifiable general duties police for several reasons.

First, because general duties police vastly outnumber specialized intelligence agents and are commonly deployed throughout the jurisdiction, they are in a better position to report suspicious activities, such as people loitering around vulnerable targets, transients appearing out of place in a particular neighborhood, or strange smells coming from clandestine laboratories (Connors and Pelegrini 2005; Riley et al. 2005). To facilitate the collection of such information as well as to alert uniformed police to possible terrorist preparations, the United States established "fusion centers" in all fifty states and several larger cities after September 11. Similarly, the London Metropolitan Police deployed counterterrorism intelligence officers in each London borough after the attack on London transport on July 7, 2005.

Second, general duties police may have contact with would-be terrorists in the course of routine law enforcement, particularly traffic stops (Finley 2006; Maguire and King 2006; Runge 2003). For example, several of the 9/11 terrorists had been stopped at some point before the attack by the police for traffic infractions. One 9/11 perpetrator had actually filed a criminal complaint with the police. In Southern California in 2005, a routine investigation of robberies at gas stations uncovered a plot to bomb Israeli government and US military installations. Narcotics detectives investigating a Mexican methamphetamine network discovered that Canadian-based pseudoephedrine suppliers were funneling money to Hezbollah.

Third, analysis of crime patterns may indicate preparations for terrorist attacks, for example, explosives smuggling, document forgery, or theft of chemical supplies (Howard 2004; Riley et al. 2005; Wardlaw 1982).

Fourth, general duties police can cultivate cooperative relations with businesses such as chemical suppliers or hospitals and with communities that may unwittingly harbor terrorists or have information indicative of precursor terrorist activity (Lyons 2002; Riley et al. 2005).

Fifth, general duties officers with extensive knowledge of local communities may be able to assess the operational validity of intelligence gathered by specialized covert operatives as well as give useful advice about how to conduct surveillance and penetration in a particular area.

Sixth, uniformed officers routinely interview criminal suspects who can be used as informants about suspicious activity or even turned into informers placed within terrorist networks (Bayley and Weisburd 2009; Richman 2004–2005).

The general lesson is that in order for regular, uniformed police to obtain useful counterterrorism intelligence in the course of their varied work, the public must be supportive of the police and willing to work with them, just as they must in the case of counterinsurgency. It requires, in short, a police that is seen to be serving and protecting the public in terms that are individually meaningful.

The London Metropolitan Police developed a program explicitly designed to do just that after 7/7. In March 2006, Operation Delphinus upgraded the duties of London's thirty-two borough commands to include counterterrorism planning, outreach, and liaison. In particular, it required them to develop community contacts, brief members of the "extended police family" about terrorism, and engage in postincident planning with local communities (personal interviews summer 2007). Within this framework, the Met developed a program called Safer Neighborhoods designed to reassure communities about their safety, take action against visible antisocial behavior, and develop contacts with local leaders that could be exploited for information about suspicious behavior. The Safer Neighborhoods program places teams typically composed of one sergeant, two police officers, and three Police Community Safety Officers (PCSOs) in each of London's 632 wards (London Metropolitan Police Service 2006; personal interviews June–July 2007). PCSOs are paid, uniformed civilians without police powers who are assigned to patrol specific neighborhoods. Although created by legislation in 2002, PCSO recruitment and deployment mushroomed in 2006. Each team develops a Key Individual Network of approximately thirty neighborhood residents who can provide leadership in emergencies and acts as liaisons for public safety planning.

It is instructive to note that even as the Met expanded its capacity to collect and analyze covert counterterrorism intelligence, it simultaneously expanded its cultivation of relationships in local communities by expanding its uniformed presence and making its personnel more easily available to serve local needs. To ensure that this deployment wasn't a short-lived gesture, Commissioner Sir Ian Blair *ring-fenced* personnel assigned to Safer Neighborhoods, which meant that they could not be assigned to other duties without authorization. Moreover, he publicly declared that in order to be successful at counterterrorism, uniformed police and specialized counterterrorist agents needed to work closely together. In his words, homeland security depends on hometown security (Blair 2007).

Although general duties police can contribute importantly to intelligence gathering for counterterrorism, their participation in covert operations is problematic, especially with respect to taking forceful preventive action. Developing a covert preemption specialization diverts resources, both material and human, from the traditional police activities of serving and protecting. Furthermore, covert operations almost always involve questionable means that, should they come to light, could undermine the legitimacy of the entire police establishment (Chalk 1996; Kaplan 2006; Lyons 2002; McVey 1997). The reputation of all police for legality, openness, and accountability may suffer accordingly. Finally, police engaging in covert operations change their mind-set from viewing the public as clients to be helped to suspects to be watched. Serving and protecting are transformed into watching and intruding.

At the same time, developing a covert capacity to prevent terrorism is hard to resist, as Bayley and Weisburd's survey shows. The public wants terrorist attacks to be prevented and are likely to fault police for not acting forcefully on intelligence at hand. Furthermore, governments often pass laws explicitly authorizing the police to be proactive, sometimes making additional money available for the creation of local counterterrorism units. Finally, general duties police already engage in covert intelligence gathering as well as preemption with respect to other forms of crime, notably narcotics and organized crime, so an expansion into terrorism seems a natural extension of their existing capacity.

The dilemma for the police with respect to counterterrorism is how to balance their usual duties—target hardening, criminal investigation, and overt intelligence collection—with those of covert preemption. One way, as we have already seen, is to create a wall between criminal investigation and covert operation. This may be facilitated if the latter are separated organizationally from other commands. Although this seems sensible, there is a contrary position that covert activities should in fact be closely connected to normal policing so that its practitioners don't develop a subculture sharply different from the culture of the organization as a whole (Independent Commission on Policing in Northern Ireland 1999). Another device is to restrict the power of arrest to the regular police, thereby preventing situations in which liberties could be withdrawn from suspects without court approval. Similarly, forceful action, however clandestine, may be regulated by law involving formal processes of authorization and review.

In summary, general duties police are very important in counterterrorism by acting in a manner that encourages the public to take self-protective action, provide reliable testimony, and share knowledge about suspicious activity. Police will inevitably become involved to some degree in covert counterterrorism—namely, intelligence collection and preemptive action. The challenge for police, then, is to exercise special care in covert counterterrorism so as not to undercut their standing with the public, which is critically important for successful counterterrorism itself. The balance thus struck is similar to that called for in COIN doctrine between military and police operations.

Crime Control

The most authoritative statement about what the police can do to control and prevent ordinary crimes such as murder, rape, assault, robbery, burglary, and theft comes from a 2004 report titled *Fairness and Effectiveness in Policing: The Evidence,* published by a panel of the National Research Council, which is a unit of the National Academies of Science (Skogan and Frydl 2004). The panel was charged with reviewing all the research on this topic since the advent of scientific evaluations of policing in the mid-1960s. It not only summarized research, but evaluated the strength of the evidence, discounting research that did not meet accepted standards.

Before discussing the panel's positive findings about what the police can do to prevent and control crime, it's important to note what they found that didn't work. The police were not successful at preventing crime when they relied on techniques of generalized law enforcement—that is, the threat or use of arrest against all forms of disorder and criminality. The strategies of generalized law enforcement, which comprised what the panel called the "standard model of policing," were hiring more officers, random patrols, rapid response to calls for service, follow-up investigations of crime, the targeting of repeat offenders, and the unfocused intensification of law enforcement. In the words of the panel:

> The standard model of policing has relied on the uniform provision of police resources intended to prevent crime and disorder across a wide array of crimes and across all parts of the jurisdictions that police service. . . . Such approaches are generally not the most effective strategy for controlling crime and disorder or reducing fear of crime. (246)

Although this was bad news for traditional policing, there was other, heartening evidence that the police could make a difference. The strongest evidence of efficacy in crime prevention involved problem-oriented policing (POP). In POP, police analyze patterns of crime in areas of persistent disorder, called hot spots, to determine if there are recurring activities that generate danger and fear. The police then determine the nature of these problems and the circumstances that create them. On this basis, they develop strategies for remedying the situations, apply them in the field, and evaluate the results (Goldstein 1990). This process has been reduced to the acronym SARA, which stands for scan, analyze, respond, assess. It has been used successfully in reducing or preventing, for example, thefts from vehicles in city parking lots, aggressive panhandling in commercial areas, robberies from gas stations and fast food restaurants, speeding in residential areas, and drug use at businesses catering to young people.

In addition to an emphasis on particular, geographically limited problems, POP involves a reliance on the regulatory and development resources of other government agencies rather than exclusively law enforcement. Examples of non–law enforcement interventions include changes in environmental design; the training of bar bouncers and apartment managers; the use of fire and building code regulations to close bars, nightclubs, and residences that generate disorder; the supply of medicine to former patients of mental institutions; periodic visits to the elderly; the reduction of truancy; and the provision of after school programs for the children of working parents.

The panel found moderate to strong evidence that intensive law enforcement focusing episodically on particular places (hot spots) can reduce such offenses as drug dealing in public parks. There was weak to moderate evidence that personal contacts made by officers assigned to permanent foot beats, as occurs in community policing, have any effect on the public's fear of crime. Community policing was devised in the 1980s in reaction to the failure of the standard model of policing. It involves consulting with communities, adapting police approaches to localities, mobilizing communities to assist police in crime control, and problem solving (Bayley 1994; 1997).

There was further weak to moderate evidence that when police treat people with respect and show regard for the principles of fairness, especially while enforcing the law, the public is more willing to cooperate and less likely to disobey the law again (Tyler and Fagan 2006; Tyler at al. 2007). Specifically, legitimacy increases when criminal justice authorities allow citizen input on street-level decisions to enforce the law and if they behave in a neutral and transparent way, are polite, and explain what they are doing. Conversely, when the police show disrespect, people are more likely to resist their authority, even engaging in acts of civil disorder. As the Independent Commission on Policing in Northern Ireland (Patten Commission) observed:

> We cannot emphasize too strongly that human rights are not an impediment to effective policing but are, on the contrary, vital to its achievement. Bad application and promiscuous use of powers to limit a person's human rights—by such means as arrest, stop and search, house searches—can lead to bad police relations with entire neighborhoods, thereby rendering effective policing of those neighborhoods impossible. (1999, 18)

If success in crime prevention involves (1) targeting people or places that are recurrent sources of illegal activity and disorder, (2) analyzing the circumstances that shape these situations, (3) developing approaches that go beyond law enforcement, and (4) mobilizing community as well as government resources as a means to a solution, then it is obvious that the public has an essential role (Tyler and Fagan 2006). Information about crime and disorder comes overwhelmingly from reports to the police from individuals (Bayley 1994; Skogan and Frydl 2004). Police knowledge of crime from their own sources is fragmentary. If the public doesn't report crimes, as is common in many countries, police literally don't know what to do, or whether what they are doing is helpful. Devising solutions to recurrent problems also requires access to the communities in which they occur. Finally, the usefulness of citizen action in preventing crime—sometimes known as *coproduction*—has been the central discovery of police research in the second half of the twentieth century. Both community-oriented policing and problem-oriented policing explicitly recognize the importance of mobilizing nonpolice resources in order to prevent crime and disorder.

Saying that the police must do more than rely on law enforcement does not mean that they should not enforce the law. Police who behave in the recommended ways are not "no powers" police. Constraining the freedom of individuals is the unique authorization given to police. The point is that law enforcement alone is not sufficient to prevent crime. There are occasions when it must be used, and the possibility of its application is a powerful prod to compliance. However, as with counterinsurgency and counterterrorism, coercion should not be used at the expense of public allegiance and support. The use of force must be balanced against legitimacy.

Conclusion

Contemporary assessments of the role of the police in counterinsurgency, counterterrorism, and crime control all emphasize the importance of developing public cooperation and support. Public participation in the creation of public safety is the great multiplier of police effectiveness. The lesson that emerges is that more than force and constraint are needed in order to win the "wars" on insurgency, terrorism, and crime. The police are best placed to provide this less forceful approach on behalf of government. They do so first and foremost by attending to the security fears and needs of individual members of the population. To rework the common phrase, police must learn to serve in order to protect. It follows that, in facing insurgency, terrorism, and crime, they must keep their priorities straight and not allow hard-edged tactics to contaminate their relations with the populace among whom they work.

4

Balancing Force and Legitimacy

> *Most assessments of counterinsurgency operations tend to ignore or downplay the role of indigenous forces and mistakenly focus on how to improve the capability of outside forces to directly defeat insurgents.*
>
> —S. G. Jones (2008)

Effective, legitimate policing is at the core of democratic nation building. Moreover, there is a strategic consensus that the most important way that police can contribute to the prevention and control of violence is by mobilizing the public to become coproducers of public safety. This is true for counterinsurgency, counterterrorism, and crime control. The police do this by responding effectively to the security fears and needs of individuals. This in turn encourages the public to take crime-preventive measures themselves; to provide information to the police about violent incidents, suspicious activities, and suspected perpetrators; and to create a moral climate of respect for law by speaking out against deviance and disorder.

In the particular context of insurgency, however, antigovernment violence may reach a level where this sort of policing cannot be developed. Insurgent violence is both the problem police may help to solve and the major impediment to police. So policymakers confront a question: how can a legitimate and effective police be developed in the face of the very violence they are crucial to preventing? Which comes first: police that effectively serve and protect the general population or the degree of safety that allows them to do so?

For the international community that intervenes in such situations, there is an added dimension of complexity, namely, what should be the division of labor between the local police and foreign security forces, both police and military? The less capable the local police are of quelling violence on their own, the greater the need for foreign military action. Furthermore, the greater the insurgent violence, the less effective the local police can be due to their own vulnerability. This is precisely the situation faced in most counterinsurgency interventions. But the greater the reliance on foreign military force, the more likely that the population will suffer from collateral damage, which may alienate them from the government on whose behalf the actions have been taken. All of this is recognized in current COIN doctrine.

For simplicity's sake, we shall refer to foreign stabilization and reconstruction as peacebuilding operations, understanding that these cover both military and police operations as well as political and economic development. Until local governments become capable of providing security, foreigners will be compelled to substitute their own forces for the local military and police. However, the more foreign forces act as substitutes for local forces, the more they undercut local responsibility for providing public safety. Furthermore, foreigners, like locals, are faced with balancing military and police activities even as they strive to build and reform local police capacities.

These problems are compounded by the fact that levels of insecurity vary over space and time within countries. Not only do different regions experience different levels of insecurity, but the whole purpose of foreign intervention is to move from stabilization and conflict mitigation to political reconciliation and economic development—and ultimately to effective, legitimate self-government. As a result, any division of labor, local or foreign, must be fluid and adjustable. What works at one place or time may not work at another.

In this chapter, we shall analyze the connections between security and the appropriate roles of the police and the military, both local and foreign. First, we will present a strategic algorithm outlining how we think determinations about these roles should be made. Second, we will explore the types of insecurity that might most affect the police role. We call this the *security continuum.* Third, we will specify the appropriate role of local police in different security environments. And fourth, we will make recommendations about the appropriate role of foreign forces, especially international police, along the security continuum.

Strategic Algorithm

Because the fundamental goal of COIN is political—namely, the creation of a self-sustaining legitimate government—the primary vehicle for dealing with an insurgency should be the police. We call this the *police primacy principle.* In counterinsurgency, the primary objective of foreign intervention is to increase local police capacity and, ultimately, reduce its own military involvement to a minimum. The military must act to create the conditions within which civilian policing can occur.

There is an important terminological issue here. Counterinsurgency confuses the distinction between police and military. It is generally accepted in Western democratic theory that the role of the military is to defend countries from foreign aggression. The police, on the other hand, are responsible for suppressing homegrown violence. By definition, then, when the military fights insurgents, it takes on an internal security role. What does it mean, then, to say that in counterinsurgency, the military and police force must be used separately and balanced? Since they can't be distinguished by the location of operation, they must be identified in other ways. We suggest that there are four characteristics that distinguish police from military operations: (1) police are more lightly armed than the military and sometimes even unarmed; (2) police customarily deploy as individuals or small groups; (3) police exercise more individual discretion in action than do members of the military; (4) police are separated organizationally from the military. They are part of a different chain of command and a different government bureaucracy.

Applying this operational definition of police, the police primacy principle means that insurgency should be controlled as much as possible by personnel deployed singly or in pairs among the population, visibly distinguishable from soldiers, trained to minimize the use of force, and capable of making decisions on their own. In the real world, however, the physical separation of military from police may not operationally be possible. Combined operations may be required, often under a single commander in keeping with COIN doctrine. But the primacy of the police should be the goal. The relationships between local police and local military, as well as between foreign and local security forces, all dependent on local security conditions, are illustrated in Figure 4.1.

The relation between the role of the police and levels of insecurity is paradoxical because it is interactive. Insecurity indicates both a need for police and an impediment to their effectiveness. Police activity impacts insurgent activity, but insurgent activity impacts what police can do. The police role is thus determined by both the requirements of counterinsurgency and the vulnerabilities deployment creates.

For each function that the police can perform, there are institutional and training requirements. These will be discussed in Chapters

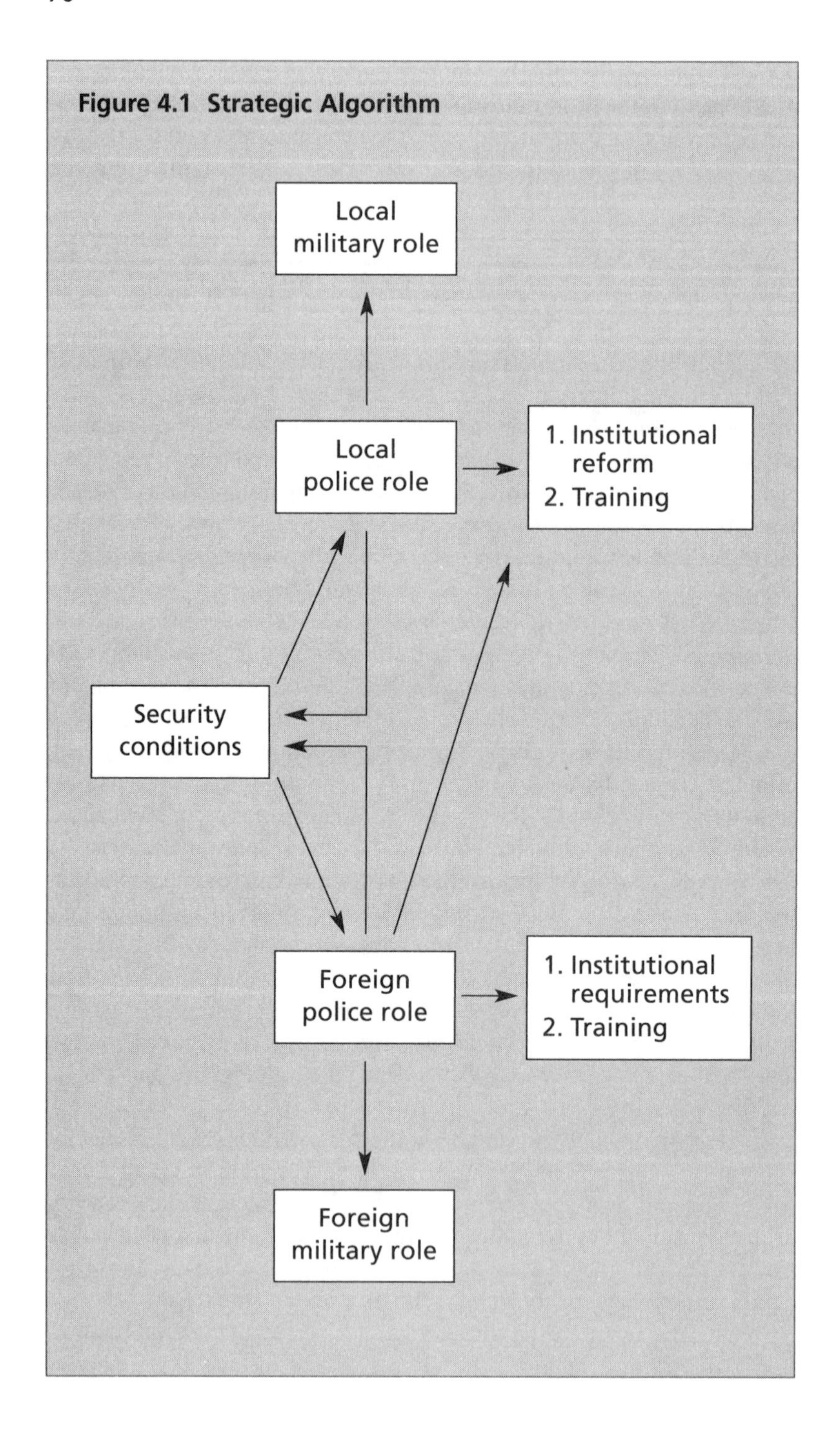

Figure 4.1 Strategic Algorithm

6 and 7. It follows that decisions about the police role must be made before embarking on organizational reform and the design of training curricula. Too often, reforms are suggested or training offered that reflects what can be given rather than what is needed (Bayley 2006).

As we have said, when the international community becomes involved in local counterinsurgencies, a corresponding division of labor must be constructed between its police and its military. Because the objective of foreign intervention is to create effective local self-government, the police primacy principle applies. International forces should privilege policing over military activity. The precise role of foreign police will depend, as it does with local police, on what the security situation allows. In the case of foreign forces, however, there is a double division of labor to consider—not just between their own police and military activities but between themselves and the locals. This too is affected by the extent and intensity of local violence. Finally, like local police, the international police require organizational support and training in order to fulfill their role. These will vary from mission to mission and may even evolve over the course of a single mission.

The Security Continuum

In their seminal book *Policing the New World's Disorder: Peace Operations and Public Security* (1998), Oakley, Dziedzic, and Goldberg point out that foreign forces face a "security gap" in the period after the foreign military gain control but before local police become effective. They suggest the creation of an interim force that has both military and police capability. In practice, this has taken the form of stability police units, modeled on the French gendarmerie and the Italian carabinieri (Perito 2003). Experience in Iraq and Afghanistan as well as in previous counterinsurgency operations shows, however, that the security gap can be more complex than the authors suggest. Decisions about the division of labor between police and military must take into account a security continuum than encompasses more than an undifferentiated gap between all-out war and ordinary criminality. We distinguish five major levels of insecurity that may be encountered in stability operations.

1. War: violence carried out by recognizable military units throughout a country in order to seize control of government. In the

context of failed states, war is civil war and it comes in two forms. It may be directed by rebels against an existing government or it may be directed by factions (racial, tribal, linguistic, religious) against one another for control of a government that is considered to be unrepresentative or unable to govern. The US Civil War is an example of the first type, the disintegration of Yugoslavia in the 1990s the second.

2. Insurgency: violence carried out throughout a country by unconventional forces seeking control of the government. This is the situation the United States and its allies have faced in Iraq and Afghanistan. Depending on its scale, insurgency may closely resemble civil war. It is often referred to as *asymmetric war* because it pits conventional against unconventional forces.

3. Subversion: episodic, unconventional, antigovernment violence, limited yet unpredictable in scope. The characteristic modes of violent subversion are terrorism and sabotage. An example of prolonged subversion is the violence committed by the Irish Republican Army in Northern Ireland and the United Kingdom mainland from 1971 to 1996.

4. Disorder: episodic, small-scale protests and agitation with the potential for violence. Disorder may take the form of protest marches, strikes, political demonstrations, and mass rallies. Its protagonists are not generally committed rebels but people with specific grievances, such as demobilized soldiers, displaced persons, ethnic groups fearful of losing customary privileges, and the unemployed (Hansen, Gienanth, and Parkes 2006). The violence in Kosovo after international intervention was largely of this kind.

5. Normal crime, including organized crime: after periods of significant violence, criminal incidents often rise as governments struggle to reestablish basic services—especially those that grow out of economic hardship, like robbery, theft, and burglary. Criminal gangs form, creating parallel systems of control in areas where the government is weak, such as slums and poorly regulated international borderlands.

These five categories of insecurity represent complex mixtures of types and severity of violence. In some countries, they may all coincide: conventional battles, cross-border incursions, assassinations, kidnappings, sporadic acts of terrorism, public protests and agitation, organized criminal activities, and ordinary crimes. This complexity makes determining the police role very difficult.

Although the security environment is perhaps the most important determinant of the police role, it isn't the only one. The decision may also depend on the political basis for conflict. For example, if violence is based on deep cultural divisions—racial, religious, linguistic—any local police will have to struggle against sectarian suspicion. Terrain, too, can affect the tactics of counterinsurgency, especially the creation of zones that are secure from attack. Capacity is another important factor in determining the role of the police. If recruits are uneducated and even illiterate, it may be difficult to train them to observe the law and serve the public. The level of local economic development can also affect the ability of the police to manage operations, communicate with personnel, and oversee performance. Finally, the ability of foreign forces to build and shape indigenous police will be critically affected by whether they are regarded by the population as helpful friends or alien foes.

Appropriate Roles for Local Police

Accepting that the role of the local police will be determined largely but not entirely by the security environment, what are the choices that policymakers face? In general, six types of police officers can be distinguished by the kind of work they perform: (1) uniformed general duties police who patrol and respond to calls for citizen assistance; (2) nonuniformed criminal investigators; (3) stability police units to control incidents of collective disorder such as strikes and demonstrations, as well as to protect police installations and personnel; (4) armed units that undertake offensive operations against insurgents, terrorists, criminal gangs, and violent criminals; (5) covert intelligence agents and analysts; and (6) border police.

There is strong agreement that police who can win the allegiance of the general population are critical in controlling violence, whether it stems from insurgency, terrorism, or ordinary criminality. The police who are best positioned to do this are general duties personnel and criminal investigators (in civil law countries this function may be shared with the judiciary). General duties officers constitute the visible presence of the police, deterring disorder and offering instant response. Criminal investigators deal with victims and witnesses and are responsible for initiating formal justice processes. By virtue of the frequency of their contact with the public, general duties officers and criminal investigators can make the greatest impact on governmental legitimacy. We shall refer to police who perform these two functions as *core police*. Their key function from a public relations perspective is to demonstrate that government can provide security and justice in response to the needs of individuals. Core police serve and protect people in order to control violence and thereby to protect governments.

In order for core police to perform their essential function of serving as well as protecting individual members of a population, they must be deployed among and be accepted by the population. Their personal safety must be reasonably assured when they patrol and when they investigate crimes. In Iraq and Afghanistan, for example, local police have themselves been the target of insurgent attacks, with recruiting stations bombed and police stations overrun. In Bosnia-Herzegovina and Kosovo, core police had to be deployed according to their ethnicity; core policing, to the extent it existed at all, was thereby stratified. The same has been true in Sri Lanka, where the national police are met with suspicion and often outright violence in Tamil areas. There are three critical indicators of whether the deployment of core police is feasible: (1) Can the police effectively serve and protect the population or will they be preoccupied with their own safety? (2) Is the magnitude of intergroup violence so great that normal police operations will often be overwhelmed? (3) Can sufficient numbers of vetted personnel be recruited to serve as core police?

These are demanding conditions. In an insurgency, violence may ebb and flow, making the decision to deploy even more difficult. Furthermore, there may be secure and insecure areas within the same country. The gradual expansion of secure areas under government control is an explicit strategy of COIN and was employed in Malaya (1954–1960), Vietnam (1966–1975), and Kenya (1955–1960) (Galula 1964; Grayling 2006; Thompson 1966). Secure areas may be extensive, as they were in Malaya, or quite small, as in the Sunni areas of Iraq until late 2007. Outside the secure areas, the military is responsible; within them, the police are. Indicators of an insecure area are the existence of no-go areas for police, the absence of people in public places, and acts of ethnic cleansing (Dagher 2007; Senate Foreign Relations Committee 2005).

Police may be especially at risk during insurgencies for two reasons: (1) they are used in military operations for which they are not trained and (2) they are deliberately targeted as representatives of government. General Joseph Peterson, the US commander in charge of training in Iraq, estimates that between 2003 and 2005, there were 12,000 Iraqi police casualties (Peterson 2006). In Afghanistan from

May 2006 to May 2007, CSTC-A reported 406 ANP were killed in action. MOI figures for roughly the same period put the count at 627 killed and 1,097 wounded (International Crisis Group 2007). Altogether in 2007, an estimated 900 Afghan police were killed (Freeze 2008).

Police are not the only ones at risk. So too are emergency medical personnel, ambulance drivers, fire fighters, damage-repair teams, and relief workers (Hartz, Mercean, and Williamson 2005). Foreigners, too, may be attacked, killed, or kidnapped, regardless of whether they are military, police, or civilian relief workers (J. L. Jones 2007). Attacks on personnel who provide humanitarian and development assistance are reported to be increasing around the world, not only in wartime. From 1992 to 2004, 218 UN civilians were killed; "intentional death" has become the leading cause of death among employees of relief and development agencies, many of which have begun employing armed guards (Spearin 2006).

Police may be at risk and incapable of acting as core police in the event not only of insurgencies but of ordinary crime, in particular the organized trafficking of narcotics and people. This is especially evident in the border states of northern Mexico and the barrios of Rio de Janeiro (Kurtz-Phelan 2008). This kind of lethal hostility is rare in the democratic West, but common in many less developed countries.

The great dilemma for policymakers, then, is how to meet shifting conditions of security without handicapping the opportunity for deploying core police who can win hearts and minds. In particular, should police themselves develop the capacity to undertake offensive operations against the perpetrators of violence or should these be left to the military?

In conditions of insecurity, the default position is against core policing. This is also true when the threat of terrorism increases and ordinary, especially organized, crime intensifies. In such circumstances, police rely more on preemptive action, indiscriminate arrest, higher degrees of force, and covert as opposed to public intelligence gathering. Command also becomes more centralized, with less discretion allowed frontline officers. This decay in core policing can be seen, for example, in 1969 to 1998 in Northern Ireland, when Republican areas were effectively depoliced, becoming no-go areas for the Royal Ulster Constabulary except under military escort.

Because the military, both foreign and local, is uncomfortable fighting unconventional wars, the great temptation is generally to substitute police for military units. Furthermore, it is easier to train local police as "little soldiers" than as "professional, accountable, public safety–oriented police" (Rosenau 2007). Initial training for police is often as counterinsurgency forces, not as "serve and protect" police. As we described in Chapter 1, the Iraq National Police was initially composed of former soldiers who were armed with military weapons and given counterinsurgency training so they could fight alongside US forces. The Iraq Police Service, which was a genuine police force, was also used in a kinetic counterinsurgency capacity, although it lacked proper training and equipment. In Afghanistan, small, isolated units of the Afghanistan National Police have been called upon to face insurgent attacks without appropriate weapons or military support. As a result, they have suffered more casualties than the Afghan military (Rosenau 2007).

In our view, local police should not be used as offensive counterinsurgency forces for four reasons. First, doing so blurs the distinction between the military and police with respect to the use of force, the rules of engagement, and accountability to the law. Second, it postpones the development of the police's crucial long-range function, namely winning the support of the local population by serving and protecting it in daily life. Third, offensive counterinsurgency operations inevitably produce collateral damage to the civilian population because they involve heavier armaments and less precise targeting. This erodes the legitimacy of the police involved. Furthermore, because both counterinsurgency and counterterrorism require preemptive action, eliminating threats before they materialize, the targets for offensive actions are potential rather than actual committers of violence. This too means the use of force is less precise, less well directed. Likewise, force used preemptively must be sufficient to overwhelm whatever weaponry insurgents or terrorists might possess. This leads inevitably to an increase in the lethality with which insurgency is met and consequently greater civilian casualties.

Fourth, counterinsurgency police forces are difficult to control. Like military units, they develop an esprit de corps that prizes operational independence. They often become a force within a force, operating according to their own priorities and stretching the limits of their legal authorization (Hansen, Gienanth, and Parkes 2006).

For these reasons, development of core police should not be delayed in favor of the creation of proactive counterinsurgency police units. Core policing comes first, not last, in forging a new police force. If offensive counterforce is required, it should be done by the military. Ultimately, police contribute to counterinsurgency by winning the allegiance of the population; the military contributes to counterinsurgency by eliminating immediate threats of violence.

Coordinating the functions of offensive counterinsurgency and population protection between the military and the police is not simple. Because levels and modes of violence are often so mixed in practice, so too will be the combinations of military and police activities (Grayling 2006). Furthermore, before police can be effectively deployed, military personnel inevitably have to perform police duties (Burack 2000; A. Hansen 2002; Pirnie and O'Connell 2008). It follows that during the insurgency, subversion, and disruption stages of violence, principles for coordinating command between police and military must be developed.

Even when police are deployed, the military may be needed to provide support in a variety of ways. In areas of extreme insecurity, military forces are required to provide force protection for the police. In Iraq, US military forces provided armored transport and armed escorts to the US civilian police advisers in the Police Transition Teams. These mixed military and civilian teams were responsible for assessing and advising Iraqi police during and after the surge in 2007 and 2008. US and Iraqi military forces were also required to protect Iraqi police stations and patrols. In Northern Ireland, for example, during "the troubles" (1969–1998) the military provided aid to the civil authorities in three ways: unarmed troops to help with natural disasters, public-order emergencies, and development projects; unarmed troops for the maintenance of essential services, especially during strikes; and armed troops in formed units to maintain public order (Ellison and Smyth 2000).

At the same time, core police dedicated to protecting local populations cannot be entirely defensive in dealing with insurgency, terrorism, and ordinary crime. Prevention is part of their responsibility, but it must be compatible with their fundamental mission of protecting the local population through the application of the criminal law. The strategic question for police in all environments is how to be effective in prevention without undermining their own legitimacy in the eyes of the population they serve.

Our argument is that the proactive prevention of violence by the use of force in insurgency environments should not be done by police. If proactive force is required, it should be done by the military as a means to support core policing, not as a substitute for it. Police development planners should privilege core policing rather than more forceful offensive capabilities. It follows as well that in areas where core police can be deployed, offensive counterinsurgency should be authorized and directed by police commanders.

If police are not to be used in forceful counterinsurgency, do they have any role to play in it beyond winning hearts and minds? They do. Police can reduce support for insurgents through the application of the law—making arrests, aiding prosecution, and meting out punishment. They can enforce regulations that hamper the development of organized insurgency, for example, the movement of people, the distribution of food, and the collection of taxes. They can collect intelligence from communities about preparations for insurgent violence. They can prevent violence by mediating intergroup disputes and tensions. They can contain incidents of violence, such as strikes, protests, and riots, which fall below the threshold of armed insurrection against the government but nonetheless contribute to disorder and fear.

Intelligence collection and analysis by the police is especially important in counterinsurgency, as it is in counterterrorism and crime control (S. G. Jones 2008). This capacity should be developed for any police deployment, with as much attention given to analysis as to information collection. At the same time, core police should not undertake covert surveillance or any intelligence gathering that detracts from their normal duties of deterrent patrol, service response, and criminal investigation. In particular, they should be careful to guard against the impression that core policing is camouflage for forceful counterespionage. Intelligence is a by-product of core policing, not its fundamental purpose.

Similarly, stability police units should not be viewed as counterinsurgency forces. Their function is the maintenance of public order, including riot control, VIP protection, convoy escorts, and the guarding of facilities. They should also be trained to perform as core police, especially patrol and rapid response, when not engaged in unit-based actions.

Finally, police cannot be expected to protect a country's borders against conventional aggression or even well-armed insurgency, but they should develop the capacity to both monitor and interdict the flow of noncombatant civilians and contraband. Because the mission of border police is specialized and restricted geographically, it should be separated organizationally from the duties of core police.

The general lesson is that when governments confront violence in any form, they should rely on police to the maximum extent possible. Police are primary, but not just any police. First and foremost, they must be core police. When core police cannot perform as called for by the strategic consensus, the military must be used. But military involvement should always be viewed as a stopgap until a police service that serves and protects the population can be reintroduced.

Because core police are so important for success in counterinsurgency, plans for their development should be made at the outset of intervention. As security conditions moderate, deployment should be expanded, but not at the expense of quality. Particular attention should be given to the retraining of police personnel who served prior to the current intervention. It is better to do core policing well in a few places than to do it badly in many. Figure 4.2 illustrates the connection between security conditions and the roles that local police should be trained to undertake.

Permissive security conditions are not, of course, the only determinant of whether core policing can be undertaken. Other important requirements include a political settlement among warring factions, the enactment of basic criminal laws, a fully functioning system of criminal justice including courts and corrections, and competent ministries of justice and the interior. The key institutional requirements for effective core policing will be discussed in Chapter 7.

Appropriate Roles for Foreign Intervention Forces

The premise of any foreign stabilization and reconstruction intervention is that locals cannot manage their own security, whether in the context of a conventional civil war or a state of lawlessness. But the form that foreign involvement takes depends crucially on the level of

Figure 4.2 Levels of Security and Local Police Roles

Security Level	Local Police Role
War	None
Insurgency	
No secure areas	Intelligence units, core police in development
Secure areas	Core police, intelligence units
Subversion	Full police services
Disorder	Core police plus stability police units
Crime and organized crime	Full police services

local insecurity. There is a variety of foreign security personnel that may be deployed.

- Military
- Military police
- Civilian police in stability police units
- Civilian police with executive authority
- Civilian police without executive authority
- Police advisers
- Police trainers

The implications of the COIN consensus for foreign intervention is clear: the responsibility for policing should be transferred to locals as soon as possible while, in the interim, foreign military operations should give way to foreign policing, also as soon as possible (Joulwan and Schoonmaker 1998). In other words, just as the local military role is derived from local police capacity, so is the division of labor between the international community's military and police forces. The higher the level of insecurity confronted by foreign forces, the greater the number of police roles the military may need to perform. Indeed, that foreign military units will perform some police functions is inevitable, be it protecting key installations, controlling access to relatively secure areas, manning checkpoints, or detaining spoilers. But the longer the foreign military are unsupported by foreign police—stability police units, operational police, advisers, trainers—the greater will become their involvement in policing. At the same time, foreign police will have a continuing need for logistical support and sometimes forceful backup by the foreign military (Hansen 2002).

Foreign police, with or without executive authority, should be trained as core police. Their function is to provide protection under law in response to requests from individuals. As with local core police, they should use force primarily to enforce criminal law or to protect themselves and others from attack. They should not be used for offensive counterinsurgency. Although they will ultimately supplant their own military, they must not serve as a substitute for it. In particular, stability police units should not be deployed as counterinsurgency forces. Their primary function is to support the core police in controlling civil disorder and responding to armed threats that exceed the capacity of individual general duties officers.

Because the development of local police is fundamental, the police primacy principle must guide the planning for stability operations from the outset, from assessing local needs to developing appropriate programs for rebuilding local forces. The deployment of advisers and trainers to the local police should occur as soon as possible. Foreign armies should not be responsible for directing police operations or training local police for two reasons. One, when military forces are used for policing, a mixed message is sent about the proper roles of military and police. Foreign stability forces must serve as role models with respect to the separation of military and police forces. Two, the military does not have the knowledge or training to develop civil policing. Civil policing requires skills and orientations unfamiliar to most military personnel, among them an emphasis on violence prevention over violence suppression, the use of minimal force to control situations, and the ability to interact with civilians.

Conclusion

The fundamental requirement for successful counterinsurgency, counterterrorism, and crime control is the presence of a government that is capable of providing essential services, including an effective police force. The key to police effectiveness, in turn, is public acceptance—in a word, legitimacy. The problem with stabilization and reform efforts, whether undertaken locally or by foreigners, is that overcoming insecurity in the short run becomes the dominant concern of policymakers. It preoccupies security personnel too, who are often most at risk in efforts at stabilization. As a result, counterinsurgency tends to emphasize forceful strategies from the beginning—military force, search-and-destroy operations, emergency regulations, covert disruption, mass arrests, and imprisonment. Short-term suppression displaces long-term development. Military force becomes the tool of choice, just as covert disruption does in counterterrorism and armed strike forces do in crime control.

This effectively undermines the strategic consensus on successful counterinsurgency, counterterrorism, and crime control—namely, that they depend in the long run on winning the allegiance and support of the population. The dilemma is to provide effective protection against a range of security threats without alienating the very population that is to be protected. Unfortunately, the legitimacy of government may be weakened both by not being effective at providing protection and by doing it too heavy-handedly.

The solution to this dilemma is to determine on the ground, in touch with operational conditions, the lowest levels of constraint and the highest levels of responsiveness necessary for effective law enforcement. This means continually assessing what police can do and need to do. In the context of counterinsurgency and nation building, the police should be viewed as primary in creating public safety, even though they cannot be relied on to do so immediately. Because the goal of foreign intervention is construction of an effective and legitimate local government, police reform must be central rather than peripheral to strategic planning.

To strike a balance between the possible and the necessary, a complicated assessment of the levels of insecurity, the capacities of local police, and the modalities of foreign intervention must be made. The various possibilities are shown in Figure 4.3. The alignments across the three dimensions are illustrative. They are neither empirically based predictions nor recommendations. Furthermore, these alignments may overlap in practice and change over time. The figure indicates what should be considered, not necessarily what must always be done.

Figure 4.3 Dimensions of Security and Modes of Control

Security Level	Local	Foreign
War		
No government	None	Military, with planning for core police
Embryonic government	Military	Military, with planning for core police
Insurgency		
No secure areas	Military	Military, with training of core police
Secure areas	Core police, with military in reserve	Military, stability police units, civilian police with executive authority
Subversion	Full police services	Civilian police, advisers, and trainers
Disorder	Stability police units	Stablity police units
Crime and organized crime	Full police service	Police advisers and trainers

5

Fundamentals of Police Training

Effective policing is as much about how the police officer does his job as what he actually does. —Richard Monk (2008)

Recognizing (1) that police play a central role in counterinsurgency, counterterrorism, and crime control and (2) that it is core police—that is, uniformed general duties officers supported by criminal investigators—who make the key contribution by enlisting the cooperation of the general public and legitimating government generally, what is the appropriate training for these crucial police officers? This, after all, is the question that prompted this book. Our answer follows in four parts. First, we stipulate the basic functions of core police. Second, we outline the training required to perform these functions. Third, we discuss the teaching methodology for core police. Fourth, we review the components of officer safety programs because, given the environments in which core police will often be required to work, they must be trained in self-protection.

After presenting the fundamentals of core police training, we examine the obstacles that trainers are likely to encounter in producing the kind of behavior that is necessary to create legitimate government. We give particular attention to the generalizability of our recommendations: is it reasonable to expect that all people in fragile and postconflict countries will react favorably to what we propose for the police?

Core Police Functions

The general function of core police is to respond to the security needs of the public as articulated through their requests for help. Training a police force to serve and protect, whether in postconflict interventions or in peaceable democracies, is not a matter of imparting technical skills. It is fundamentally a matter of changing attitudes about the work of policing, emphasizing above all the importance of being available, helpful, and fair and respectful.

Being Available

Core police must learn to act democratically in the sense that they must respond to the needs of individuals. Advisers from first-world countries, which are the foremost contributors to stability operations, may not understand how unusual it is for police to be available to requests for service from individuals. In most of the world, the police are hard to contact, unhelpful in response, and predatory. What they do is determined entirely by directions from government communicated through appointed senior officers. They are not the public's police; they are the government's (Bayley 1985). The public thus does not expect that in instances of crime or disorder the police will come quickly, listen carefully, and act accordingly.

Police can make themselves available in several ways. They can be contacted in person at their bases, such as police stations, outposts, or offices. This requires police agencies to assign to these bases officers who have been trained to be sympathetic, who are knowledgeable about standard operating procedures, and who are willing to act promptly. Availability is further enhanced by creating police facilities that are easy to enter, reasonably comfortable to visit, and where privacy is provided as needed.

In Sarajevo, Bosnia, for example, the entrance to the central police station was remodeled to make the building more inviting to citizens seeking assistance from the police. A glass door was installed so visitors could see into the building. In the lobby, a brightly colored waiting room with comfortable chairs was provided. There was also a desk with chairs for visitors that was manned full-time by a policewoman in uniform who was prepared to direct inquiries to the appropriate offices as well as to receive complaints about the police themselves.

Police should also be proactive in their availability, leaving their stations, buildings, and offices to move among the population and actively welcome requests for help. Indeed, it is on the streets where most people see police, especially if they patrol on foot or by bicycle rather than in cars or vans. In countries where telephones are common, contact needs to be facilitated by publicizing toll-free emergency numbers. In countries where telephones are the primary mode of contact, it may be necessary to create a nonemergency number for questions of a strictly informational nature—about the law, government services, or the progress of an individual's case. Handling both kinds of telephone calls requires staff who are carefully selected and trained to make prompt referrals to operational police as well as to other governmental and nongovernmental agencies.

Finally, police should actively solicit input from the public at meetings held in community facilities at convenient times. These meetings may be with the residents of a particular neighborhood or with business owners, set in schools or hospitals, or coordinated with special interest organizations, such as homes for battered women or homeless shelters. Police should also designate officers to meet regularly with communities that feel they have been particularly neglected or mistreated by the police, such as racial and ethnic minorities, immigrants, and displaced persons.

Availability is more than a matter of positioning. It is an attitude. Officers must show by their voices and bearing that they are approachable, that a request is not an imposition but an opportunity to help. Interaction can also be encouraged by small patrols of one or two officers and by de-emphasizing the display of weapons.

Being Helpful

It is not enough for the police to be available to the public. They must also respond in a way that is seen to be helpful or at least sympathetic. Being helpful in many cases involves intervening to "handle-things-that-shouldn't-be happening-and-somebody-should-do-something-about" (Bittner 1970). It doesn't mean solving all problems, but it does mean restoring order and preventing things from getting worse. To be helpful, then, police officers must learn what they can and can't do in terms of law and policy. Because police are often the first responders to reports of crime, they should be knowledgeable about elementary criminal investigation. If they serve in a liaison capacity to groups or neighborhoods, they should also learn how to assess problems of crime and disorder with people in the community and to devise solutions. In short, being helpful is more than an attitude of willingness; it requires knowledge and communication skills.

Even so trained, officers cannot be helpful if the organizations in which they work do not provide the time for them to do so. If police officers are always under orders from which they can't deviate or assigned to static posts they cannot leave, they will be unable to provide responsive service no matter how well trained. Being helpful is a matter of managerial facilitation as well as training.

Being Fair and Respectful

The heart of core policing is treating the public with fairness and respect, as clients to be served rather than as potential troublemakers to be controlled. Police must be taught that although they will be required to enforce the law, sometimes through force and constraint, their primary job is to encourage people in need to come forward and to ask for help. Unfortunately, in countries that need core policing the most, the police themselves are usually viewed as troublemakers. Since in those places, things get worse, not better, when police become involved, people contact them only when it can't be avoided or as a tactic to be used against others for personal advantage. To change this perception, police must be trained to act firmly but courteously, to be open-minded and slow to judge, to be tolerant of social diversity, and to be respectful of the rights of everyone.

The three defining attributes of core policing—availability, responsiveness, and fairness—are very similar to what has been called *community policing* (Bayley 1994; Skolnick and Bayley 1988; Trojanowicz and Bucqueroux 1990). It too aims to build links to communities in order to enlist the public as coproducers of public safety. Unfortunately, the community policing movement has been imprecise about its operational activities. Although community policing certainly encompasses being available, helpful, and fair, it has been extended to so many other features of policing, including particular physical facilities, specialized units, and organizational changes, that many police officers have become skeptical about it. The phrase has also been overused, in some places quite cynically in order to appear democratic and progressive. For example, even repressive governments, such as China and the former Soviet Union, have required communities, work places, and schools, to cooperate with police. But enforced mobilization by the government is not community policing. Genuine community policing, like core policing, requires the police to make service to the public their fundamental strategy.

Community policing as developed over the past twenty-five years should be viewed as a refinement in the general movement toward service and protection. Western advisers who tout community policing abroad tend to forget that it has developed in their own countries on top of a tradition of policing that was already distinctively available, responsive, and increasingly fair. Without this foundation, the implementation of community policing is difficult if not impossible.

The Core Curriculum

Devising a curriculum for core policing isn't a matter of installing a whole new system in place of the old. The new curriculum needs to be adapted to what is usable from old practices. This means studying how policing is customarily done and assessing the capacities of personnel to deliver what is lacking. In particular, the curriculum should never be a mechanical copy of training that is done in other cultural and economic circumstances. The curriculum should reflect what needs to be done locally in order to build an effective, legitimate police force.

The curriculum we recommend has ten modules, covering four general topics, as follows.

1. Introduction to Core Policing
2. Legal Framework
    - Police mandate
    - Criminal law and procedure
3. Skills of Service Delivery
    - Facilitating requests for assistance
    - Principles of effective responding
    - Handling crimes: victims, witnesses, and evidence
    - Working with community groups
    - Problem solving
4. Fundamental Values
    - Ethical conduct
    - Equal treatment

The following description of core policing modules is not intended to be an instruction manual for trainers. That would require a great deal of detail about the number and length of sessions, required reading, visual aids, guest speakers, lecture content, writing assignments, breakout groups, discussion exercises, role playing, and so forth. We will, however, make suggestions later about the pedagogy needed for teaching the core curriculum.

Introduction to Core Policing

This involves thoroughly exploring the reasoning set out in this book, namely that core policing is smart policing against insurgency, terrorism, and violent crime. In particular, that core policing is fundamental to the reduction of violence and the construction of legitimate government, that public support and cooperation raise the effectiveness of the police, and that police are crucially placed to convert the public from passive onlookers or active foes to coproducers of public safety.

Legal Framework

Police need to know what they are authorized by law to do. This is fundamental to creating the rule of law. Core police must also be told clearly how they are expected to act in carrying out their mission—their objectives, priorities, and standards of behavior.

Skills of Service Delivery

Facilitating requests for assistance. Instructors should review experience locally as well as abroad for ways to make contact between police and public easier and more attractive. Recruits should be encouraged to draw from their own experience and that of their friends and families in discussing discourteous treatment by police and then asked to pinpoint how the police could become more welcoming and more responsive to requests for assistance.

Principles of effective responding. Core police should explore the range of requests that local people may make for police help. In particular, they must understand that it is not only crime that needs to receive police attention but situations in which immediate action is required to avoid conflict, injury, and distress (Bittner 1970). Students should receive special training in defusing interpersonal conflict, calming emotions, and taking charge of potentially violent situations. They should also be trained in referring people to other agencies, private and public, for legal advice and counseling about personal matters that cannot be handled by police.

Handling crimes: victims, witnesses, and evidence. Because responding to crime is at the heart of the police mandate, core police need to know how to assist victims, encourage witnesses, and preserve physical evidence. Depending on local laws and practices, they should be clearly instructed in the local division of labor between uniformed police and criminal investigators. For example, can uniformed patrol officers make arrests, take statements, or compel attendance of witnesses?

Working with community groups. As part of their duties, core police should share information about crime patterns with the public, discuss persistent local problems, and solicit community help. Thus they need to learn how to conduct public meetings and make presentations. Even if this work is assigned to crime prevention specialists, core police should understand what is involved so they can work supportively.

Problem solving. If this task is assigned to core police rather than to specialists, they should be instructed in what has become known as problem-oriented policing. Although the problem-oriented paradigm has been modified in practice from place to place, it basically involves four activities: scanning instances of crime and disorder for underlying problems; analyzing the reasons for these problems; responding to the problems with well-devised programs of action; and adjusting the programs as needed for greater effectiveness (Eck et al. 1987; Goldstein 1990).

Fundamental Values

Ethical conduct. Core police should be taught that their powers are subject to law. Particular attention should be given to restrictions on the use of force and constraint. Officers should also understand the disciplinary rules of their own organization and the procedures that will be followed in case of violations. Finally, core police need to be taught how to encourage complaints from the public about police misconduct and what the procedures are for dealing with them.

Equal treatment. In many ways this is the most sensitive subject core police must confront. Discussions of social divisions—religious, racial, linguistic, ethnic—are often considered taboo in police training, particularly in countries emerging from ethnic or sectarian conflict. These divisions and the prejudices they engender need to be addressed during training so that police from different groups can work together and provide a model of reconciliation for the community. At the police academy in Kosovo, for example, ethnic Albanian and Serb cadets were required to share rooms in the dormitory and to undergo special training that explored their attitudes toward other ethnic groups in the context of their obligation to help reunite their society.

Officers cannot provide equal protection under the law if they do not recognize their own prejudices and compensate accordingly. Programs should be devised to sensitize officers to the common humanity of people across social divisions. Although this can be done in part through classroom presentations, it is more effective through informal interaction between police and members of different communities, especially when they occur on the home-ground of minority communities.

Special attention should be given to the needs and vulnerabilities of women. For example, it is important for officers to understand that violence against women is most likely to occur in domestic settings and that victims may be unwilling or forbidden by custom from discussing it with male officers (Denham 2008). Treatment of women may be improved through the recruitment of more than a token number of women and involvement of women in all aspects of policing.

The general lesson is that police powers must be used in the service of everyone, regardless of background. Conversely, no favoritism should be shown in policing, whether on the basis of social status, political power, or money.

These modules do not constitute a complete curriculum for the basic training of core police. Core police also need to be taught how to use firearms, write reports, operate communications equipment, drive vehicles, and administer first aid. They must also learn the routines of patrol, criminal investigation, crime-scene preservation, arresting and detaining, and traffic regulation. Finally, they should gain experience in the types of situations they will most often be called upon to handle, such as disputes among street vendors, domestic violence, runaway and abused children, drunks, and drug addicts.

It is critical, however, that these professional skills not be developed at the expense of changing the orientations of police recruits. Priorities must be kept clear. The policing that generates legitimacy in peacebuilding missions cannot be achieved through making local recruits as skilled as police officers in donor nations. What has made policing "democratic" and respected in Western countries isn't the ability to handle computers, crime-scene forensics, defensive driving, and the routines of patrol. It is the civic sensibilities toward law, government, and public service that personnel bring to the job. Western policing can afford to emphasize techniques and technology. Peacebuilding nations cannot. The principles of core policing must not only receive priority in training but permeate the entire curriculum, even the most technical aspects.

Teaching Advice

In order to teach these topics successfully, especially the ones dealing with the delivery of police services, instructors should begin with what their students already know about local policing. The subject of core policing should be situated within their knowledge of how police have customarily behaved. They will thus be more likely to understand why the new curriculum is important. In effect, the recruits themselves can be used as informants with respect to improving public regard for the police. They might be asked, for example, how citizens could help the police reduce crime and the fear of crime—and why they don't currently do so. Or they might be asked to specify, based on their own experiences, police actions that leave a bad impression.

Instruction needs to be practical rather than theoretical. Although the rationale for the new curriculum needs to be taught, it should relate directly to the working lives of police officers given different assignments. One good example of how to be available, responsive, or fair in a typical encounter is worth a thousand admonitions. At the same time, it would be naive to think that training, especially when it marks a sharp break with the past, can be accomplished in a few drills and lectures. To be effective, training must be lived, involving a combination of formal instruction, practice, and operational experience. Most important, the obstacles encountered by trainees in the field in adhering to the new norms must be confronted explicitly by training personnel, with strategies devised for coping with them.

The implication here is that instruction needs to be interactive. It should stress dialogue between trainers and recruits, with questions always encouraged. Lectures can present themes, but discussions should follow that explore operational implications and, in particular, students' doubts about their abilities to perform as needed given their level of education, prior experience, or social background. The new curriculum will, almost inevitably, be delivered against the grain of police tradition and public expectation. Police officers, old and new, need to voice their own reservations before taking to the streets.

No matter how interactive instruction may be in the academy, it needs to be reinforced by practice. The only way to close the gap between formal instruction and its application in the real world of policing is to require new officers to work in operational settings, especially in patrol and response units, under the supervision of carefully selected field training officers who have been vetted for their understanding of and commitment to the new program. These officers should be specially trained in how to interact with police cadets and provided with a field-training curriculum of lectures and exercises that reinforce what recruits have been taught in the classroom. They should be encouraged to report to the police academy about the readiness of graduates to perform basic police functions so that deficiencies in training can be corrected and adapted to real world requirements.

Trainees should then return to the academy to discuss the problems they encounter in practicing what has been preached. As with trainees worldwide, their initial exposure to the working world of policing will make them wonder whether they can live up to the precepts taught. Senior officers need to hear these doubts so that they can better manage the implementation of core policing. At the same time, trainees need to be taught how to be effective in applying what they have been taught against both the reality of the street and the attitudes of long-serving officers. Most important of all, the period just prior to graduation should be used to create a bond of mutual support, of group identity, among the new core police. They should emerge from it believing that they are, in effect, leaders of a critical social transformation.

Officer Safety and Survival

In environments where the police are themselves primary targets of violence by insurgents, terrorists, or organized criminal gangs, they cannot be expected to perform as needed unless they are able to protect themselves. Although the responsibility for combating generalized, recurrent, and organized violence falls mainly to the military, its efforts to clear areas of insurgents and prevent infiltration may not always shield police from violent attacks. These may take the form of ambushes on patrols or attacks on facilities. In Afghanistan, for example, approximately a hundred police have been killed each month since January 2007 (US Government Accountability Office 2009). The US Department of Defense estimates that combat losses have been three times higher for the Afghan police than for the Afghan military. Even if such violence occurs infrequently, it may cause police to become preoccupied with their own safety and to neglect protecting local populations. In order to reassure police in such unpredictable circumstances, training must address how violence may be anticipated, avoided, and confronted.

Following the logic of police deployment discussed in Chapter 4, basic safety training should focus on defensive anticipation and protection, not offensive tactics and capabilities. Offensive operations may be required for specialized police units such as SWAT teams, stability police units, and counterinsurgency strike forces, but not core police. In order for this to work, senior commanders in charge of public security—both military and police, local and foreign—must determine when conditions are sufficiently benign that core policing can be successfully done. This is one of the most difficult decisions that commanders face, but it is essential to the development of legitimate policing and, hence, legitimate government.

A bare-bones course in officer safety has been developed by the US Department of Justice's International Criminal Investigation and Training Assistance Program (ICITAP). Spanning five days, including two days of practical exercises, it covers (1) anticipation and survival tactics; (2) field movement, contacts, and cover; (3) traffic stops; (4) domestic disturbances; (5) building searches; (6) pat downs, body searches, and prisoner restraint; and (7) prisoner transport.

A much more extensive program in officer safety has been created for local police in Iraq and Afghanistan (CPATT 2008). Instruction in survival skills, defensive tactics, and weapons handling accounts for 59 percent of basic training, or 236 of 400 hours over the course of ten weeks. The curriculum consists of the following modules and topics.

1. Survival Skills (137 hours)
   A. Module 1 (fifty hours)
      - Patrol objectives, response, and radio communications
      - Principles of use of force
      - Tactics for avoiding fatal errors
      - Force continuum
      - Shoot-don't-shoot
      - First aid: assessment, breathing, CPR, triage, bleeding, shock
      - Cover, concealment, and firing positions
      - Defense of police installations
      - Handcuffing, prisoner restraint, and prisoner control
      - Prisoner transport
      - Personal off-duty protection
   B. Module 2 (forty hours)
      - Deployment, weapons use from vehicles, ambush, and field of fire

- Vehicle checkpoints
- Vehicle stops
- Vehicle searches
- Vehicle identification
- Contact and cover
- Extractions

C. Module 3 (forty-seven hours)
- Contact and cover
- Patrol and weapons handling
- Building searches
- Patrol, fire, maneuver, and ambush
- IEDs, bombs, and cordons

2. Defensive Tactics (forty hours)
- Use of force and survival skills
- Balance and movement
- Team building and communication skills
- Handcuffing, suspect search, and escort
- Hard empty hand techniques
- Dynamic takedowns and suspect control
- Weapon retention and disarming
- Police baton use
- Physical fitness and conditioning
- Exercise testing

3. Weapons (sixty hours)
- Firearms safety and introduction to AK-47
- Disassembly/reassembly and maintenance
- Weapons handling
- Weapons manipulation
- Marksmanship
- Introduction to Glock 9mm
- Handgun safety
- Six fundamentals of marksmanship
- Weapons handling
- Assembly/reassembly and maintenance
- Range and low-light shooting: AK-47 and Glock 9mm (thirty-five hours)

There is a good deal of repetition among these modules. Much of the training focuses on the use of force and, depending on how it is taught, dovetails with both the law and ethical conduct sections of our core police curriculum. The emphasis on weapons training, especially

AK-47s, reflects an offensive capability not in keeping with core policing. One can't fault the necessity for such training in Iraq and Afghanistan, but the fact that it was deemed necessary reinforces the importance of making correct decisions about when core policing can be undertaken. At the same time, officer safety programs must be balanced between reassuring officers about their ability to protect themselves and not exaggerating the dangers they face. This is delicate. Officers must be protected, but in doing so the impression should not be created that they are going to war. War is not their business.

Officer safety programs are not a distinct, well-defined package. One size does not fit all. Operational commanders must decide which self-protection skills their core police should have. They can be given too much or too little. The deployment of core police involves subtle, complex decisionmaking. So too does the adaptation of officer safety programs to different environments.

Impediments to Successful Training

Training in core policing is fundamental to creating behavior that engenders the support of the population. It faces enormous obstacles, however, in changing the behavior of police. Even when well done and in benign environments, the effect of training on police behavior is limited and declines over time (Lonaway, Welch, and Fitzgerald 2001). Some impediments are within the ability of a determined police leadership to overcome; some are not.

First, reform cannot be brought about through training alone. Reform cannot be led from the bottom. It requires management from the top. Furthermore, to make a difference, the lessons acquired during training need to be used on the job. Unfortunately, because organizational tradition often prevails, newly minted trainees quickly discover that what they have been taught is dismissed by veterans as impractical or faddish (Bayley 2006). If core training is to succeed, every rank needs to be trained in its responsibilities as regards implementation. It is instructive that when the British retrained the Malaya police during 1952 and 1953 in the midst of an insurgency, they provided a three-to-four month advanced course for all commissioned and noncommissioned officers and sent dozens of promising senior commanders to Britain for a full year of instruction (Thompson 1966). In short, organizational practice determines the extent to which training affects behavior on the job (Mastrofski and Ritti

1996). The solution is to train police managers in the value and techniques of core policing. It follows that the training of managers in core policing must precede training rank-and-file police.

Training in support of core policing must be designed for different managerial levels (Hansen 2003). To simplify slightly, there are three levels: first-line supervisors who monitor operational behavior, middle managers who implement programs, and senior executives who devise programs and represent the organization externally (Lunney 1998). Each of these positions has different responsibilities for facilitating core policing. First-line supervisors must be trained to gauge the effectiveness of core strategies as practiced and to coach core police on the job. Middle managers must learn to design implementation plans as well as criteria by which to judge the performance of core police. Senior executives must understand thoroughly what core policing involves and its contribution to effectiveness in countering insurgency, terrorism, and crime. They must be able to explain its value to their own personnel as well as to relevant stakeholders outside the police organization.

Second, training in core policing will have to struggle against the inherited culture of the police organization. For example, police may believe that in order to be respected they must be authoritative, direct, and forceful. Criticism from citizens may be considered unacceptable, a mark of disrespect that must be met with punishment. Traditional police management may also be anti-intellectual, even unscientific, relying on "common knowledge" and gut-instinct more than empirical analysis and evaluation. If core policing is to become the operational paradigm, attitudes such as these must be confronted and changed.

Third, the culture of the organization may discourage the development of the qualities required for core policing, in particular, individual initiative and responsibility for taking appropriate action. Simply put, in many police organizations, subordinate officers are taught to defer to the authority of their superiors. They are neither considered capable of making decisions nor encouraged to value personal responsibility over obedience to commands (Pfaff 2008). Conformity to commands rather than responsibility to objectives is the operating rule. In Iraq, for example, lower ranks, including sergeants, are treated as servants by their superiors, who require them to perform personal services and allow them to act only on command. Real policing, in American terms, is done only by lieutenants and above. According to interviews we conducted with US trainers in

2008, senior Iraqi officers see little need to train the lower ranks at all, let alone in core policing. This outlook is not uncommon in the world. It can be found throughout South Asia, the Middle East, and in the former republics of the Soviet Union.

Fourth, a job in the police may be viewed by everyone, police and public, as an opportunity to be exploited for the benefit of the officers themselves, their families, ethnic groups, or friends. Failure to do so may be seen as strange, even disloyal. One US officer who served in Iraq observed that police officers "are not viewed as an individual but rather as a member of a community, whether it is family, clan, or tribe" (Pfaff 2008). These interests take precedence over the abstract and unfamiliar goal of using authority for the shared interests of the population as a whole.

Fifth, the alienation of the public from the police may be profound. In many countries, especially where insurgencies occur, the public views the police as unresponsive, corrupt, and brutal (UN Development Programme 2001). Police engage in false arrests, accept bribes, steal, threaten, blackmail, use illegal drugs, and collude in crime. They harass vendors, confiscate documents, rape women who register complaints, beat innocent suspects, torture, and kill. As Rachel Neil has said, "In much of the developing world, [police] are Janus-faced: as instruments of coercion and control they are often supremely powerful; as agents of protection and development they are often profoundly weak" (Neil 1999). In such circumstances, it will take years for citizens to accept the promises of new policing.

Sixth, the core curriculum may have to be integrated into very different systems of police education. In the United States, for example, general education is provided outside police academies in high schools and colleges. Training in operational issues, such as a core curriculum, is added afterward. In Europe, however, police training is often combined with secondary and university-level education in schools run by the police themselves, who may even award master's and doctoral degrees (Marenin 1996; Pagon et al. 1996). Some of these institutions are similar in function to US military academies. In all police educational systems, however, basic training in some form is given to recruits, supplemented later by in-service training for upgrading skills required for promotion and mid-level supervisory responsibilities, and advanced training for special skills and senior management functions (Kratcoski 2004).

Seventh, educational levels of police vary hugely around the world. While the core curriculum outlined here may seem straightforward to people in developed countries, it will be hard to teach in places where recruits can barely read and write. In Afghanistan, for instance, where 70 percent of the population is illiterate, the inability of police recruits to understand even the most simple textbooks and manuals means that trainers have had to develop special educational materials and methods of instruction. Moreover, foreign trainers are often required to teach through interpreters in languages not their own. This doubles the time that training takes—or, to look at it another way, halves the time available for instruction absent the need for translation. It also requires foreign trainers to spend time working with their interpreters to ensure that technical terms are understood, foreign concepts are correctly translated into local cultural terms, and appropriate local examples are found for illustrating police objectives and practices.

Training modules cannot be taken off the shelf in donor nations and applied with any expectation of success in many of the countries in which peacebuilding will be done. While peacebuilding trainers will inevitably draw on what they know from home, any curriculum, including this one, needs to be reexamined and adjusted to fit local organizations and cultures. This means that intervention forces should not plunge into training straight off the plane. They must reconnoiter, assess, and adapt. This requires time and sensitive diagnostic skills.

At the same time, it is important to state unequivocally that lack of education itself is not an impediment to the creation of core policing. Core policing doesn't require high-level technical skills. It is a matter of attitudes. A college degree is not required to understand how to become available to individuals in need, how to respond in helpful ways, and how to treat everyone equally. These are commonsensical and, as we shall argue shortly, resonate in the life experiences of people around the world.

The obstacles that core policing faces are not intellectual; they are organizational, managerial, and cultural. Although training is essential, by itself it has little chance of success of changing traditional attitudes and practices. Training alone is a blunt instrument for transforming police organizations.

Will Core Policing Work Everywhere?

Following the logic of counterinsurgency doctrine, we have argued that the essential function of local police in environments of transitional security is to serve and protect the population. Thus, we argue, local police must be trained in what we have called core policing, the essential elements of which are availability, responsiveness, and fairness. The question that naturally arises is whether this makes sense for all countries in which counterinsurgency may be encountered. Is core policing appropriate in countries that do not share the cultural orientations of Western countries?

Research in the United States has shown that how people are treated by the police, especially whether it is perceived to be respectful and even-handed, affects not only their regard for the police but the likelihood that police actions will be accepted (Tyler et al. 2007). Fairness consists of being given an opportunity to state one's case, to react to information that authorities possess, and to be treated with dignity. In short, the legitimacy of legal authorities is enhanced if they demonstrate that they are sincere in striving to be fair and just in their dealings with individuals. Police who are perceived to be legitimate are less likely to encounter physical resistance to their actions and, consequently, are less likely to be injured (Tyler et al. 2007). The broader implication is that acceptance of the rule of law depends not only on the substance of decisions but how justice is administered by all agents in the justice system:

> When the public views government as legitimate, it has an alternative basis for support during difficult times. Further, when government can call upon the values of the population to encourage desired behaviors, the society has more flexibility in how it deploys its resources. In particular, it is better able to use collective resources to benefit the long-term interests of the group, since they are not required immediately for ensuring public order. (Tyler et al. 2007, 26)

Although most international police observers would agree that people everywhere are likely to respond favorably to the strategies of core policing—and especially its emphasis on procedural fairness—direct evidence from outside the United States in the form of surveys, before-and-after studies, and systematic observation is fragmentary (Tonry 2007). Procedural fairness in the exercise of authority by both the police and the courts has been shown to be associated with legitimacy in the Netherlands, Germany, the former Soviet Union, Japan, and South Africa (Tyler at al. 2007). According to surveys, procedural justice was the most highly rated legal value in five European countries—Bulgaria, France, Hungary, Poland, and Spain—in 1995 and 1996 (Cohn and White 1997). But apart from these studies, research has not demonstrated that the desire for procedural fairness is universal.

At the same time, we do know that lack of legitimacy is a global problem. For example, studies in Mexico, Brazil, and South Africa suggest that when governments fail to provide security and justice, people resort to individual and community forms of self-defense. Moreover, people around the world agree about the ranking of what should be considered serious crime—murder, rape, assault, robbery (World Values Survey 2008).

Crime is viewed as a problem almost everywhere and crime increases as countries emerge from conflict (Bayley 2006). In its 1999 survey of crime internationally, the UN's Office of Drug Control and Crime Prevention found that two out of three people in cities were victimized at least once over a period of five years. Twenty percent of these victimizations involved serious crime: robbery, assault, and sexual assault (1999).

Public opinion surveys in several countries emerging from civil war show that fear of crime is commonplace. For example, a large random-sample survey taken in Iraq in 2008 showed that crime was ranked as the third most important problem for people personally, after poor electricity and unemployment (D3 Systems and KA Research Ltd. 2008). Four years earlier, in 2004, Iraqi respondents had ranked crime the number one problem, more serious than insurgency or terrorism (Center for Strategic and International Studies 2004). Similarly, in Afghanistan, a 2006 survey by the Asia Foundation showed that crime was considered to be the biggest problem the country faced, followed by unemployment (Asia Foundation 2006). That same year, 47 percent of people in El Salvador said they felt unsafe or somewhat unsafe (Latin American Public Opinion Project 2007). While in South Africa in 1999, five years after the creation of the postapartheid government, people thought fighting crime ought to be the country's second-highest priority after unemployment (Rule 2000). Twenty percent had been the victims of crime in the preceding year; 35 percent thought the government had no control over crime.

There is also compelling evidence that people in less developed countries, regardless of cultural traditions, distrust the police. The 2008 World Values Survey showed that 67 percent of US citizens had a great deal of respect for the police, as compared with 63.5 percent of people in Bosnia-Herzegovina, 56.5 percent of South Africans, and only 38 percent of Indians. A 1999 survey by the UN's Office of Drug Control and Crime Prevention showed that only 20 percent of serious crime victims in Latin America and Africa reported the offenses to the police. These regions were particularly low by world standards. A majority of crime victims felt they had no one to turn to for help. Furthermore, less than 50 percent of people who reported crimes to the police were satisfied with the response. The lowest levels of satisfaction were found in Latin America, Africa, and East and Central Europe. A 2006 survey of Latin America showed that 70 percent of victims would not notify the police (Latin American Public Opinion Project 2007). Surveys such as these suggest that there is a need that is not being met by the police.

With respect to fairness, corruption by public servants is seen to be widespread in most countries, but especially in less developed countries. In El Salvador, for example, 43 percent of people surveyed considered corruption pervasive (Latin American Public Opinion Project 2007). In Afghanistan, 42 percent of respondents reported encountering corruption in daily life. The higher the level of government in question, the greater the expectation of corruption: 50 percent implicated provincial governments, 62 percent suspected the national government (Asia Foundation 2006). Moreover, it is the police who are viewed worldwide as the most common source of corruption (NOETIC Corporation 2008).

Although studies like these show that relief from crime is a high priority worldwide, they do not show how people judge the performance of the police. Is it by level of crime, behavior of the police, quickness of police response, or punishing guilty offenders? In particular, would people in non-Western, underdeveloped countries emerging from conflict welcome increased access to police, more responsiveness, and greater fairness? We don't know. At the same time, it would be a mistake to assume that people in postconflict countries wouldn't value police availability, responsiveness, and fairness simply because they have different cultural traditions. It would, indeed, be condescending to presume so.

We propose a test for this, one we have carried out in several Third World countries. What do parents teach their children to do when the children are away from home and need help? When we have asked this question of general as well as police audiences, we find that people accept the question as fair, a valid indicator of the standing of the local police. Our experience, then, impressionistic rather than scientific, suggests that legitimacy depends on whether the police are regarded as reliable friends at moments of need. Not on the objective incidence of crime, not even on personal fear of crime, or success of the police in catching criminals. Legitimacy depends, as US research suggests, on personal assessments of how police treat people, particularly when people need help, whatever it may be.

Conclusion

Granting that core policing is fundamental to counterinsurgency as well as counterterrorism and crime prevention, how much time should be devoted to it in basic training programs? Core police training should extend over twenty-six weeks at a minimum: sixteen weeks at a police academy, seven weeks of on-the-job training tutored by an experienced officer, and one week back at the academy for debriefing and a review of the basic lessons. As we will see in Chapter 6, this is much more than is being given to recruits in Iraq and Afghanistan at the time of this writing in 2009. It is, however, similar to the curriculum in Bosnia-Herzegovina and Kosovo. Basic training for police in the United States takes twenty-six weeks on average. European basic training takes from sixteen weeks to four years, depending on how it is combined with elements of secondary or tertiary education (Pagon et al. 1996). Perhaps most instructive of all, during the insurgency in Malaya in the early 1950s, the British stopped all offensive operations in order to retrain the entire police force in a four-month program (US Army/US Marine Corps 2007). Considering the ambition of any plan to create a legitimate, population-serving police where none has been before, twenty-six weeks should be considered the minimum time period in which to accomplish so much.

As we have seen, many things need to be covered in basic training in addition to availability, responsiveness, and fairness—for example, officer safety, operational tactics for different situations, administrative procedures, physical fitness, and local history and culture. We suggest the following proportions in terms of classroom instruction.

- Core policing: 25 percent
- Officer safety: 25 percent
- Situational tactics: 30 percent
- Physical fitness: 13 percent
- Administrative procedures: 3.5 percent
- Local history and culture: 3.5 percent

Although officers of all ranks must receive training in core policing if the orientations involved are to become institutionalized, instruction in technical skills—such as criminal investigation and traffic management—might be stratified by rank. Lower ranks would be viewed primarily as first responders, responsible for stabilizing situations and calling for skilled backup as needed. They need not be trained as all-purpose police officers, capable of handling every eventuality. As the visible face of policing, lower ranks need to display the orientations of core police. Such stratification of function would reflect the organizational culture of many countries in which there are peacebuilding missions.

It is essential to remember that core police training cannot be imparted solely through formal lectures and presentations. Its three fundamental strategies must inform all aspects of training, especially officer safety and situational tactics (Independent Commission for Policing in Northern Ireland 1999; Oversight Commissioner 2000–2007). Core policing is not a set of techniques; it is an orientation to the job. It can be done by people who are otherwise unskilled; it can even be done by people who are illiterate. Training in core policing is not an add-on to technical skills. It comes first. It follows that the shorter the time allowed for basic training, such as the standard ten-week program in Iraq and Afghanistan, the greater the proportion of time that should be devoted to core policing.

Although changing the orientation and practices of police in the circumstances encountered in peacekeeping is dauntingly difficult, there have been success stories: in Northern Ireland after the Good Friday Agreement of 1998, in the Punjab state of India after the Sikh independence movement of the 1980s, in post–civil war El Salvador (1992), in South Africa after apartheid (1992), in the United States during the Progressive era of the early twentieth century, and in Germany and Japan after World War II. Reform will never be quick or assured, but it can happen. The police can be taught to serve and protect rather than exploit and repress.

Core policing is the armature on which the legitimation of government hangs. Success in its development requires specialized training and, simultaneously, broad organizational facilitation.

6
World Practice in Police Training

Capacity building is a long-term, relationship-based activity, rather than simply a menu of trainings of skill sets to be delivered.
—M. Malan (2008)

If the purpose of peacebuilding is to develop sustainable, effective, and democratic governments, then local police play a central role in achieving that objective. They do so through actions that demonstrate to the population that the new or reformed government is worth supporting. Police accomplish this, we argue, by responding to the security needs of individuals and doing so in ways that are fair and legal. The key to training police for this purpose is the inculcation of new orientations toward the police function, not simply learning the technical skills of law enforcement. We call this core policing. The implementation of programs to develop core policing should begin from the first moment of foreign intervention.

Against this prescription for police training in peacebuilding, we now examine what has actually been done by the United States and other international donors in recent stabilization and reconstruction missions. First, we review the content of training programs in a selection of major interventions since the early 1990s: Iraq, Afghanistan, Bosnia-Herzegovina, Kosovo, and Timor-Leste. Second, we compare these programs with our own training prescriptions for core policing. Third, we discuss the impediments to describing and evaluating police training programs undertaken by the United States and other international donors. Fourth, we review the difficulties in implementing international police training missions, paying particular attention to the training that foreign advisers receive.

Content of Training Curricula

We will examine recruit training programs from five contemporary peacebuilding missions: Timor-Leste in 2003, Iraq in 2006, Afghanistan in 2008, Bosnia-Herzegovina in 2008, and Kosovo in 2008. The difficulties of constructing a larger sample will be discussed later.

Police training institutions report their curricula in terms of major categories of subject matter, with specific courses or modules listed under each. In Iraq, those categories are (1) democratic policing, (2) crime, (3) antiterrorism, (4) survival skills (a three-part course), (5) defensive tactics, and (6) firearms. Figure 6.1 shows the ten-week basic training curricula for recruits in 2006 (CPATT 2006).

Although the length of the training program has varied during the mission in Iraq from two weeks to ten weeks, its content has not. With small changes in the amount of time devoted to different categories, the 2006 curriculum has become standard: 10.8 percent of the time is devoted to democratic policing, 10 percent to criminal investigation, 20 percent to antiterrorism, 34 percent to survival skills, 10 percent to defensive tactics, and 15 percent to firearms. Clearly, US trainers have been preoccupied in Iraq with police protection, constituting almost 80 percent of total training. Although law enforcement skills courses are to be found under other headings, they too are oriented to officer safety.

In Afghanistan in 2006, recruits to the Afghan National Police were trained for eight weeks in twenty-nine separate subjects (Department of Defense 2006):

- Introduction
- Hygiene
- Values and ethics
- Afghan constitution
- First aid for basic trauma
- Penal code
- Criminal procedure code
- Use of force
- Empty hand techniques (soft and hard)
- Handcuffing and person searches
- Human rights, prohibition against torture, human trafficking
- Handling prisoners
- First responder responsibilities

- Domestic violence, family assistance and women's rights
- Community policing, democratic policing
- Traffic laws, commercial vehicles, control, investigation
- Defensive baton method
- Immigrant law
- Official documents, passports, IDs
- Drug awareness and investigation
- Checkpoints
- Hazardous materials
- Police station security
- Civil disturbance
- Explosive devices and bomb scenes
- Drills
- Physical fitness
- Firearms: rifle qualification and pistol familiarization
- Tactical training

Grouping these courses as best one can into the five categories found in Iraq, the time devoted to democratic policing is 11.2 percent (compared to Iraq's 10.8 percent), crime 17.6 percent (Iraq 10 percent), antiterrorism 2.8 percent (Iraq 20 percent), survival 21.2 percent (Iraq 34 percent), defensive tactics 20.3 percent (Iraq 10 percent), and firearms 15.9 percent (Iraq 15 percent). Although specific antiterrorism training was markedly briefer in Afghanistan than it was in Iraq (2.8 percent versus 20 percent), the bulk of training was again devoted to force protection and officer safety (60 percent versus 79 percent). Afghan recruits did, however, get almost twice as much training in criminal investigation as did Iraqi police (17.6 percent versus 10 percent).

At the time of this writing in 2009, the basic training curriculum throughout Bosnia and Herzegovina, including the ethnic-Serbian entity known as the Republika Srpska, is a twenty-five-week (or 1005-hour) course (European Police Mission 2008). This program is administered under the supervision of the European Union, which replaced the United Nations in that capacity in 2003. It would have been informative to compare the present curriculum with that designed by the United Nations in 1996–1997, but the material is not available. Indeed, describing iterations in police training provided by foreigners in almost any intervention mission is impossible, as we shall explain in more detail later.

Figure 6.1 Iraq Basic Training: Ten-Week Curriculum

Block 1: Democratic Policing	*43 Hours*
Introduction	1
Democratic policing	1
Organizational structure	2
National disciplinary code	2
Police ethics	2
Systematic approach	2
Communications skills	2
Human rights and the Iraqi police	8
Human rights and prohibition against torture	2
Gender issues	2
Diversity awareness and hate crimes	2
Community policing	2
Health and stress management	2
Equipment accountability and responsibilities	1
Leadership and team building	2
Physical fitness training and conditioning	10
Block 2: Crime Module	*40 Hours*
Crime categories and criminal attempts	2
Criminal liability and lawful excuse	1
Crimes against persons	1
Crimes against property	1
Crime accessories	1
Crime scene management	10
Use of force	2
Justification	2
Apprehension	4
Roles of the judiciary and search procedures	4
Domestic violence	2
Physical fitness and conditioning	10
Block 3: Antiterrorism	*80 Hours*
Introduction to terrorism	1
Intelligence awareness	2
Police briefings	2
Hostage survival	3
New surveillance and security	2
Terrorist tactics used in Iraq	8
Explosive devices	6
Suicide bombers	4
Small arms and ambush	3
Explosive hazards and awareness training	24
Reaction to ambush and contact	5
Physical fitness and conditioning	10
Practical exercises, scenario training, testing	10

(continues)

Figure 6.1 continued

Block 4: Survival Skills	*50 Hours*
Prepatrol operations	1
Enforcing curfew	1
Pedestrian stops	1
Patrol procedures	4
Custody procedures	2
Emergency radio and Barrett radio procedures	10
Silent communications	2
Use of force	1
Personal survival	2
Officer safety	3
Basic first aid	6
Cover, concealment, fire and maneuver	3
Prisoner management	1
Building and police station security	2
Physical fitness and conditioning	10
Block 5: Survival Skills II	*40 Hours*
Police survival	8
Advanced first aid (combat)	10
Permanent vehicle checkpoints	2
Temporary vehicle checkpoints	2
Vehicle searches	8
Physical fitness and conditioning	10
Block 6: Survival Skills III	*47 Hours*
Contact and cover	1
Foot patrol, weapon handling, fire and maneuver	12
Building search: practical exercises	6
Contact and cover: practical exercises	6
Responding to ambush	6
IED bomb explosions	6
Physical fitness and conditioning	10
Practical exercises, scenario training, testing	
Block 7: Defensive Tactics	*40 Hours*
Use of force and police survival skills	2
Balance and movement	2
Team building and communications skills	2
Handcuffing, suspect searches, escort	6
Hard empty hand techniques	3
Dynamic takedowns and suspect control	2
Weapon retention and disarming	3
Police baton use	6
Physical fitness and conditioning	10
Exercises and testing	4

(continues)

Figure 6.1 continued

Block 8: Firearms	*60 Hours*
Firearms safety and introduction to the AK-47	3
Disassembly/reassembly and maintenance	3
Weapons handling	2
Weapons manipulation	3
Marksmanship	3
Performance and objectives: Glock 9mm	1
Handgun safety	2
Six fundamentals of marksmanship	1
Weapons handling	2
Assembly/reassembly and maintenance	2
Range shooting: AK-47 and Glock 9mm, low-light shooting	35
Course Total	*400 Hours*

Source: CPATT 2006.

Training time in the Bosnia-Herzegovina curriculum is distributed as follows:

- Police duties and code of conduct: 16 percent
- Police weapons: 9 percent
- Criminology: 9 percent
- Traffic safety and driving instruction: 10 percent
- Special physical education: 12 percent
- Physical culture and first aid: 9 percent
- Psychology: 3 percent
- Constitutional establishment and system of state administration: 4.5 percent
- Criminal and misdemeanor code: 7 percent
- Human rights: 3 percent
- IT and communications: 9 percent
- Foreign language: 6 percent

In the relatively benign security situation of Bosnia-Herzegovina today, less attention is given than in Iraq or Afghanistan to force protection and defense (9 percent) and more is given to law enforcement skills (47 percent) and the law itself (14.5 percent), including human rights. Instructors devote almost equal time to formal presentations (52 percent) and practical/situational exercises (48 percent).

In Kosovo in 2008, a twenty-week (or 800-hour) course of recruit training is organized into four blocks of subject matter, plus physical exercise and drills (Kosovo Police Training School):

- General policing: 37 percent
- Operational police skills: 12.8 percent
- Firearms: 9 percent
- Traffic matters: 5 percent
- Exercise/drilling: 36.2 percent

"General policing" refers to a miscellany of courses covering operational procedures, criminal investigation, administration, law, human rights, democratic policing, and discipline. "Operational police skills" include officer safety and defensive precautions. In Kosovo as in Bosnia-Herzegovina, force protection is not a major preoccupation, allowing twice as much time to be given to training in law enforcement values and skills.

The basic recruit training program for Timor-Leste was developed in 2003 (Australian Federal Police 2008). It consists of 704 hours of training over a four-month period distributed as follows:

- Administration: 2 percent
- Democratic policing: 7 percent
- Humanitarian aspects: 0.4 percent
- Investigation procedures: 14 percent
- Patrol procedures: 0.8 percent
- Policing skills: 42 percent
- Legal issues: 22 percent
- Assessment, drill, and ceremonies: 12 percent

The bulk of the curriculum is devoted to basic skills, including patrolling, criminal investigation, and procedures such as report writing, prisoner handling, traffic direction, map reading, and computer use (57 percent). This includes ninety hours of firearms training (13 percent) and forty-five hours of instruction in officer survival and use of force (6.5 percent). The curriculum is notable for the attention given to democratic policing (7 percent), which covers codes of conduct, ethics, human rights, community policing, and problem solving. This is in addition to the 154 hours devoted to law (22 percent). Forty-four percent of training is done in classrooms; 56 percent in practical exercises and scenarios.

The length of recruit training varies enormously in our sample among training missions, depending largely on the security situation, from eight weeks in Afghanistan (as of 2008) to twenty-five weeks in Bosnia-Herzegovina (2008). In both Iraq and Afghanistan, basic training was more rushed at the beginning of the intervention when security was especially problematic. Figures on the length of training, whether counted in weeks or hours, can, however, be misleading. If training is not given in the local language, as is usually the case when led by foreigners, effective training time should be reduced by half to account for consecutive interpretation. Every statement by instructors must be translated, as must responses from students. Consequently, a program that looks like eight weeks will actually be only four. Furthermore, time should be deducted for induction orientation, program administration, and graduation. Trainers we have talked to say, for example, that an eight-week program in Iraq not given by Iraqis themselves, amounts to no more than three-and-a-half weeks of actual instruction.

According to our sample, except in the cases of Bosnia-Herzegovina and Kosovo, the duration of recruit training is much shorter than similar training in the major donor countries. As Darrell Stephens, a former US chief of police and consultant to the US military, says, "Unfortunately, the tendency seems to be one of a relatively short formal training period, with the expectation [that] recruits will pick up what they need in the field" (Stephens 2008). By contrast, basic police training in the United States lasts twenty-six weeks; in Australia twenty weeks, in Canada twenty-four weeks at minimum, in the UK thirty-one weeks, and in Sweden two years. Classroom instruction is then followed by extended periods of field training under the supervision of experienced officers and reinforced by a return to the classroom for short periods of review. Such hands-on operational training occurs in our foreign sample only in Bosnia-Herzegovina and Kosovo. Not only are programs in donor counties longer, they are conducted under optimum security conditions with educated and highly motivated recruits who speak the instructor's language and understand the social norms and historical traditions that underlie the curricula.

Core Policing in Contemporary Training

The descriptions of the five preceding recruit training programs are based on the major categories of subject matter we identified in curriculum documents. Each category, however, contains many courses, some of them grouped more by convenience than intellectual relevance. This is especially true for the categories of democratic policing and crime/criminology. In the Iraq curriculum, for example, what falls under the rubric of democratic policing includes the structure of the police, communication skills, and health and stress management. In order to get a more accurate picture of the content of recruit training, we have compared the subject matter of individual courses, using a template composed of six subjects covering fifteen topics, which is presented in Figure 6.2.

In the template, we mark the elements we consider requirements for training in core policing—namely, democratic policing; law, including disciplinary regulations; use of force; and strategies to enhance availability, responsiveness, and fairness. To qualify as democratic policing, courses must cover the goals and purposes of policing in a democratic society. We separate the study of democratic policing from instruction in local legal codes. The major problem in this scheme is the category of police operations, which includes courses that cover the handling of encounters with citizens, including criminal investigation procedures and tactics in the use of force. Some of this instruction clearly impacts whether recruits are helpful and responsive in ways that the public appreciates. By omitting these courses, we may be underestimating the attention given to the manner of police response.

Although comparing curricula by course titles is better than comparing them by general subject matter, the resulting judgments about intellectual content may still be inexact. Course titles may, for example, not reflect what is actually taught. Furthermore, the material covered in one course—for example, the principles of the use of force—may be raised again in other courses, especially those devoted to handling particular kinds of situations. In other words, more instruction may be given on particular topics than an enumeration by course titles suggests. The only way to escape from the problem of mistaken classification and repetition in teaching would be to dig down another level and inspect lesson plans. Unfortunately, these are even harder to obtain than curriculum overviews. Lesson plans may also not reflect what is

Figure 6.2 Curriculum Categories for Comparing Course Titles

1. Fighting capability
   A. Physical fitness and conditioning
   B. Marching and military protocol
2. Law
   A. Human rights[a]
   B. Constitution; criminal law and police law[a]
   C. Discipline and procedures[a]
3. Police operations
   A. Tactics and situational skills: stops, checkpoints, searches
   B. Handling crime: crime scenes, evidence collection, interrogation, victim handling
   C. Use of force, nonfirearms: handcuffs, batons, chemical sprays[a]
4. Officer safety
   A. Defense
   B. Weapons training
   C. First aid
5. Orientations
   A. Democratic policing and rule of law[a]
   B. Availability: community policing[a]
   C. Responsiveness: problem-oriented policing[a]
   D. Fairness/ethical conduct[a]
6. Local history and culture

Note: a. Elements we consider requirements for training in core policing.

actually being taught. Instructors often differ in their delivery of content depending on their own knowledge and comfort with particular subject matter. Ultimately, then, the most reliable way to get an exact accounting of the content of training in any country is to monitor instruction as it is given. Since this was not possible, auditing by labels at some level of generality had to suffice.

The recategorization of curricula by course titles is shown in Figure 6.3, using the 2006 curriculum for Iraqi recruits as its example. Readers are invited to compare our analysis of course-level distributions with the broader analysis shown in Figure 6.1.

Applying our course-based template for comparing recruit training across the sample of five contemporary programs, we conclude that officer safety in the form of anticipating and avoiding serious risks accounts for as much as one-third to one-half of training in insecure environments. Coupled with firearms training, officer safety easily takes up half of all training for recruits, especially in countries where security is problematic. It also appears that courses explicitly titled "Defensive Tactics" and "Officer Safety" have grown over time in both Iraq and Afghanistan. Explicit training in the principles of the application of force as opposed to weapons use is rare, amounting to less than 5 percent. Moreover, "use of force" often covers more than firearms, in particular the use of handcuffs and methods for unarmed

Figure 6.3 Iraq: Ten-Week Recruit Training Program, 2006

	Hours (T = 400)	Percentage of Curriculum
1. Fighting capability	120	30
A. Physical fitness and conditioning	60	15
B. Military marching: protocol	0	
C. Weapons: familiarization and shooting	60	15
2. Law	18	4.5
A. Human rights[a]	10	2.5
B. Crime, penal, police[a]	5	1.2
C. Disciplinary procedures[a]	2	0.5
3. Police operations	93.2	23.3
A. Tactics, situational skills	51	12.8
B. Handling crime	26	6.5
C. Use of force[a]	16	4
4. Officer safety		
A. Defense (including 70 hours of antiterrorism)	116	29
B. First aid	16	4
5. Orientations	11	2.75
A. Democratic policing and rule of law[a]	1	0.25
B. Availability: community-oriented policing[a]	2	0.5
C. Responsiveness: problem-oriented policing[a]	2	0.5
D. Ethics[a]	6	1.5
6. Local history and culture	0	0

Note: a. Indicates relevance to core policing.

control and self-defense. These are often referred to as soft or empty hand techniques.

The next most substantial part of the curricula, amounting to about a quarter of all course time, consists of standard operational instruction: searching buildings, stopping-and-frisking, taking statements from victims of crime, house-to-house canvassing, searching motor vehicles, dealing with domestic violence, confronting armed robbers, setting up roadblocks, and preserving crime scenes. The emphasis in this category is on ensuring that encounters with the public are both legally justified and physically safe for officers. Very little time, less than 7 percent, is spent on the skills involved in criminal investigation. This is appropriate considering that the training we sampled is for recruits, not for detectives, and in countries where the uniformed rank and file are not expected to do criminal investigations or, indeed, almost any task that involves judgment. Physical conditioning accounts for almost as much training time as the development of professional skills. Some of it takes the form of marching and indoctrination into military protocol.

Instruction in local law—constitutions, penal and procedural codes, police powers—follows operational training and physical education in importance, but distantly, usually constituting less than 10 percent of class time. The Bosnia-Herzegovina academy in Sarajevo is unique in that, at the time of this writing in 2009, it devotes almost a third of its curriculum to local law. Timor-Leste is also an exception, devoting 22 percent. Explicit training in international human rights may be a part of law modules, but it is a much smaller part than instruction in local law. Hardly any instruction is given in discipline—codes of conduct, adjudication procedures, and the reporting of complaints.

Across our sample, combined training in what we have identified as core policing—human rights, the use of force, discipline, democratic policing, availability, responsiveness, and fairness—accounts for less than 20 percent of any recruit training program if one excludes training in local law. In the 2006 Iraq curriculum, for example, only thirty-seven hours (or 9.2 percent of the curriculum) are devoted to what might generously be called core policing—namely, to courses designated by them as democratic policing, police service discipline, human rights, gender, diversity, communication skills, and leadership and team building (see Figure 6.3). In Afghanistan, it is 16.7 percent, in Bosnia-Herzegovina 19 percent, in Kosovo 10.3 percent, and in Timor-Leste 15 percent. Training in availability, when it is provided at all, consists entirely of community policing. Practices that increase responsiveness are never taught explicitly, unless rare courses in communication are included.

Not only is responsive behavior not taught, but the situations recruits are instructed in handling are those generated proactively, that is, by the police themselves (building searches, stopping-and-frisking, searching motor vehicles) rather than reactively from public requests for service (house burglaries, sexual harassment, quarrelsome neighbors). The one exception is domestic violence. In other words, police are prepared to some extent for the work they initiate but not for the services that individuals might request. Training is for directed rather than responsive policing.

There is no clear association between instruction in core policing and the security environment. Training in core policing is slighted in both Iraq and Kosovo, yet it is emphasized in Bosnia-Herzegovina and Timor-Leste. In both Iraq and Afghanistan, attention to core policing appears to have declined over time in favor of self-defense and weapons handling. Iraqi trainers, who have gradually replaced their US counterparts, have also placed greater emphasis on military protocol, such as marching in formation and other elements that were part of police training under Saddam's regime.

In summary, instruction for recruits in peacebuilding missions currently emphasizes self-protection, including the use of firearms, and technical skills; service-oriented instruction is an afterthought. If instruction in local law is included in core policing—as one might well argue it should be, given the importance of the rule of law for policing in general—then the time devoted to core policing goes up substantially in all countries except Iraq.

Iraq	10.4 percent
Afghanistan	25.7 percent
Bosnia-Herzegovina	34.0 percent
Kosovo	18.3 percent
Timor-Leste	37.0 percent

Hardly any documents discuss the methods of instruction appropriate for recruits, although Timor-Leste, notably, conducts almost half of its training through practical exercises and scenarios. Nor do many mention the need for supervised training in the field before certification as police officers. The program in Bosnia-Herzegovina is an exception, where the pressure to deploy officers quickly has abated.

Until the Department of Defense was given responsibility for police training in Iraq in 2004, peacebuilding operations were conducted by the US Justice Department's International Criminal Investigation Training Assistance Program (ICITAP) under guidance from the Department of State. In 1999, ICITAP designed a five-week course titled "Basic Police Skills" for the Kosovo Police School, which was gradually refined by the staff of international instructors and expanded to eight weeks. The subjects in this curriculum have become standard for US government police training programs, appearing wherever the United States has been involved. Analyzing the ICITAP curriculum on the basis of its component courses, we find the same pattern as that in our five-case sample.

Fighting capability (entirely familiarization) — 17.0 percent
Law (including human rights at 12.5 percent) — 18.5 percent
Police operations (including use of force at 9.5 percent) — 43.5 percent
Officer safety — 11.2 percent
Orientations (democratic policing 2.5 percent, community policing 1 percent, ethics 5 percent) — 10.0 percent

No time at all is devoted to the history of conflicts or to local cultures. The importance of changing the fundamental strategies of policing is, once again, barely acknowledged. The ICITAP curriculum does, however, stress the importance of interactive instruction, using practical exercises, simulations, and projective scenarios.

Impediments to Curriculum Comparison

Our conclusions about what is being taught to local police in peacebuilding missions are based on an admittedly small sample. This is because information about curricula is very difficult to obtain. At the time of this writing in mid-2009, no major donor country maintains libraries of foreign police–training curricula, not even for those programs they may have sponsored or participated in developing. None of the US government departments and agencies involved in developing and delivering training in peacebuilding missions had such collections. Not the Departments of State, Defense, or Justice. There were not even lists of curricula developed within specific missions, which might have indicated how training has evolved over time. This lack of documentation is particularly disappointing considering that the US government undertook police training in a systematic way as long ago as 1986 with the creation of ICITAP, which developed curricula for Panama, El Salvador, Somalia, Haiti, Bosnia-Herzegovina, Kosovo, Timor-Leste, Iraq, and Afghanistan. Furthermore, although the State Department has paid contractors an estimated US$6 billion through its Bureau of International Narcotics and Law Enforcement for police training in Iraq alone since 2001, it does not have a collection of the programs it has paid for. In the memorable words of one former military adviser we interviewed, the Defense Department also does not have a "belly button" that military personnel can push to produce documentation about curricula in previous missions. In short, the US government has no institutional memory about the content of the police training programs it has utilized in peacebuilding missions.

The US government is not unique in this respect. Other major donors, such as the UK, Australia, and Canada, cannot produce descriptions of the training in which they have engaged. The UN Department of Peacekeeping Operations, which in the mid-1990s explicitly broadened its police mandate to include advising and training, also cannot produce the curricula used in any of its over twenty subsequent missions. The same is true for the Organization for Security and Cooperation in Europe, which has been involved with police training in Bosnia, Kosovo, Eastern Europe, and the republics of the former Soviet Union.

There are two major reasons why training curricula have not been collected by sponsoring governmental institutions. First, because civil reconstruction has been underresourced, the administration of police training has been rudimentary and ad hoc. Moreover, civil administrators have been so busy putting "boots on the ground" that they haven't had the inclination to do the record keeping that could guide future efforts. In short, agencies have failed to hire the information specialists (librarians) who can build institutional memory. Second, contractors involved in the development of training programs view their work as proprietary, part of their comparative advantage in the market for funding. Universities might be expected to serve as depositories for government-developed curricula, but they can't collect what hasn't been made available.

With the exception of the basic training program for Timor-Leste, therefore, all the curricula we analyzed were provided either from the foreign training academies themselves (as with Bosnia-Herzegovina and Kosovo) or from the private files of individuals we know personally who served in missions, particularly in Iraq and Afghanistan. However, as might be expected with material that "fell off the back of the truck," it was often so uneven in quality that it could not be compared. Curriculum outlines were not standardized in form, were incomplete or lacking in detail, or reflected training expedients unique to particular times and places. Our sample of five programs represents the most detailed curricula we could find.

It would also have been informative to chart the modifications in curricula as security conditions changed in the countries we examined. Unfortunately, the surprising and very disappointing inadequacy of documentation in the intervention period made this impossible. Without firsthand experience, it would also be difficult to determine whether modifications were made due to changes in the environment or as a belated response to problems long recognized. In other words, causal analysis of changes in training over time would require getting into the minds of successive managers.

The lack of institutional memory about police training among all donors, multilateral as well as bilateral, has two important consequences. First, without benefit of previous experience, trainers have to reinvent the wheel again and again. If the trainers have been police themselves, they draw on their experience at home, transferring it to the local context. They may also reach out to colleagues who have served in similar missions. Second, the donors are unable to describe or evaluate systematically what they are doing. More importantly, they have no information about what works best in various contexts.

For an enterprise that is considered fundamental to postconflict stabilization and reconstruction, the failure to document police training is inexcusable. Nor should the participation of contractors, whether for-profit or not-for-profit, be allowed to prevent the open, collaborative discussion of police training in peacebuilding. The allocation of public money requires open competition and public accountability.

Training for Trainers

It is axiomatic that training is only as good as the people delivering it. Curriculum outlines show the thrust of training, but not whether the content is being taught competently or even whether it is being taught as advertised. That determination would require observation on the scene by persons qualified to judge. This was beyond our capacity and has, to our knowledge, not been done in any mission. Nor, indeed, has the impact of training on students been studied, either in terms of cognitive retention or subsequent behavior.

Although we lack direct information about both what is being taught and its impact, we do know a great deal about the background of foreign advisers and the preparation they receive. Until 2004, US training for indigenous police forces in postconflict interventions was carried out exclusively by civilian law enforcement personnel provided and funded by the State Department, either through private contractors or by ICITAP in the Department of Justice. The personnel deployed were largely civilian police officers from federal law enforcement agencies (FBI, DEA, Marshals Service) or officers either retired or on-leave from state and local agencies. Such instructors were deployed in Panama, El Salvador, Somalia, Haiti, Bosnia-Herzegovina, Kosovo, and, initially, in Afghanistan and Iraq. In 2004, however, responsibility for all aspects of reconstruction in Iraq was given by presidential order to the Department of Defense, which also took over in Afghanistan in 2005. These orders overturned long-standing policies against the US military engaging in the training of foreign police (Perito 2007). This does not mean that military personnel have wholly replaced US civilians as trainers in Iraq and Afghanistan, only that training is subject to military direction. The United States continues to recruit civilians to serve as police advisers and instructors through the Department of State, which now acts as a subcontractor to the Department of Defense.

The United States is unique in deploying civilian police to peacebuilding missions who are not government employees but are selected and paid by private contractors. At the time of this writing in 2009, all police training in Iraq and Afghanistan was done by DynCorp, under contract to the Department of State through the Bureau of International Narcotics and Law Enforcement. Although funded by the US government, DynCorp's two-week predeployment training program is not a matter of public record, but is considered proprietary. According to interviews with former DynCorp recruits, training consists mostly of orientation to the contract, logistical preparation for deployment, and familiarization with administrative procedures. The rest concerns defensive tactics and weapons use, with perhaps a day devoted to local culture. Almost no attention is paid to the tasks that must be performed in the field. Once deployed, DynCorps personnel get additional briefings locally. Reports from the field suggest that US military police get more predeployment instruction in the tactics of mentoring and instructing local police than do the DynCorps contractors with whom they serve in Police Transition Teams.

The transfer of foreign police training to the US military has resulted in a change in doctrinal emphasis. Whereas the Department of State and ICITAP stressed democratic policing along with the investigation and criminal prosecution of terrorists and insurgents, the Department of Defense views local police as auxiliaries in support of "kinetic" counterinsurgency operations. The army and marine counterinsurgency manual, although acknowledging the importance of local police in winning hearts and minds, stipulates that police should be trained particularly in weapons handling, small-unit tactics, special weapons, convoy escorts, riot control, prisoner handling, police intelligence, and station management (US Army/US Marine Corps 2007, 231–232). In effect, the US military continues to view local police as "little soldiers," contributing primarily to offensive counterinsurgency and counterterrorism, force protection, and intelligence collection (Rosenau 2007).

Current American COIN doctrine postpones for an undefined time the development of the sort of local police who can respond to the security needs articulated by the general population, design responsive crime-prevention strategies, and deliver impartial justice.

Few foreign trainers from any country, be they civilian or military, receive instruction in the design and delivery of police training. They are selected primarily for their experience as operational police officers. Demonstrated skill in teaching is not a selection requirement for foreign deployment anywhere. Peacebuilding missions act as if deploying people with operational experience is sufficient for inculcating new norms and procedures.

The same is true in multilateral missions. The UN Division of Police, located within the Department of Peacekeeping Operations, has not developed a generic model of training for indigenous police. During peace operations, police assigned to training functions are expected to devise training curricula appropriate to local conditions. As a result, programs vary widely among missions, based as they are on the programs of countries from which the training officers have been recruited, and may change radically as UN personnel rotate through missions. Predeployment training for police personnel is the responsibility of contributing states, although the UN has developed a curriculum spanning two weeks (ten working days) that is given at regional training centers or by member states. It consists of thirty training modules mostly devoted to information about UN missions, with particular forcus on personal security and standards of conduct, and substantive topics such as human rights, civil-military coordination, community policing, and child protection (UN 2008). The closest its curriculum gets to instruction in training are very short modules on "cultural awareness," "reform, restructuring, and rebuilding of law enforcement," and "mentoring and advising" (UN 2008).

UN ability to reconstruct indigenous police with an orientation toward democratic law enforcement and the rule of law, let alone toward the strategies of core policing, is limited not only by a lack of direction and predeployment training but by its recruitment process. The UN's largest contributors of police personnel, such as Bangladesh, Pakistan, and Nepal, have some of the worst records on the global Foreign Policy Human Rights Index, while countries with the best records, like Sweden, Spain, and the United Kingdom, are relatively small contributors (NOETIC Corporation 2008). The same is true with respect to measures of political instability and governmental corruption for major donor countries. If advising, training, mentoring, and coaching are supposed to lead to the strategic reorientation of local police in peacekeeping missions, UN personnel are dubious exemplars.

It should be noted that some countries have gone beyond barebones, narrowly focused training for police deployed to peacebuilding missions. The Australian Federal Police provides a mandatory thirty-five days (or 296 hours) of training for police personnel recruited for foreign deployment from its several state police services as well as its own ranks. Building on the UN's recommended modules, the Australian program adds instruction in teaching, advising, and capacity building, including cultural sensitivity, coaching, and community development. The Swedish National Criminal Police has added a police commanders course to the UN's basic predeployment course. Sweden has also developed a unique one-week course for both police and civilian personnel titled "International Police Development," which is designed to develop the skills needed to manage police reform and reconstruction (Swedish National Criminal Police 2008).

In addition to instruction in how to teach, police advisers to peacebuilding missions must be prepared to confront three endemic issues that can affect their ability to train local police. They are (1) the anticipated level of violence, (2) cultural norms concerning the law and police authority, and (3) traditions excusing unprofessional behavior. Many police advisers, especially those from developed countries, have never been the direct targets of violence by insurgents, terrorists, or even violent criminals; any casualties incurred on their part have by and large been the result of interventions to stop violence among others. Self-defense training is therefore not only important for their own sake but for those they train, whose risk of encountering violence they must estimate. If they can't do this and acknowledge it in their instruction, they will appear naive and out-of-touch to their students.

They must also adapt their training to the enforcement norms of different populations. For example, Australian police deployed in Timor-Leste discovered that young protesters didn't obey commands to stop but instead ran away and then threw stones (Goldsmith 2009). Foreigners need to think carefully about what it means to restore law and order in such contexts. In Goldsmith's words, "Upholding the 'rule of law' in post-conflict and fragile societies may mean a reassessment of Western policing priorities."

Finally, foreign trainers need to understand how to confront behavior that is customary by cultural tradition but is contrary to the standards being taught. Colonel Tony Pfaff, who served two tours in Iraq, observes that in order to succeed at reform, foreign trainers need to understand the social constraints under which local police operate (Pfaff 2008). Resistance to reform may not stem from a failure to understand the norms but social pressure to ignore them. Trainers need to think carefully about when they should defer to tradition rather than insisting on reform. This is especially true with respect to corruption. At the same time, Pfaff says, although foreign advisers may have to tolerate some institutional latitude in behavior, they must never fail to confront abuses, including corruption, that occur in their presence (2008). Trainers should never seem to be saying "Do as I say, not as I do." In short, training has its tactics too, which are critically important to the success of training missions. They need to be explored in practical terms as the trainers themselves undergo training.

Conclusion

Despite substantial investments of money, the training of local police overseas in peacebuilding missions remains a phantom activity, known to exist but hard to see. Training curricula are not systematically collected by any government or multilateral organization. They are not available to help in planning new missions or to guide would-be trainers on the ground. And they are never evaluated in terms of impact.

Substantively, current programs neglect the essential elements of legitimation. They are preoccupied with counterforce operations as well as officer safety. This emphasis blurs the distinction between military and police functions, a distinction that most donors consider fundamental to democratic policing. In US peacebuilding missions, the distinction is further blurred because civilian participation has been subordinated to military direction. Moreover, the length of training is unacceptably short by the standards of the very donors who are supplying it.

Finally, the people recruited to train local police abroad are themselves untrained in curriculum design or pedagogy. They are also unprepared to adapt their instruction to local conditions, especially those of insecurity on the one hand and cultural norms on the other. Police reform abroad will not occur by copying foreign procedures or by telling "war stories," regardless of the degree of operational experience that trainers have. Training and mentoring require special skills and the ability to adapt them to different environments. Successful training abroad begins with better training at home.

7

Institutional Reform: The Larger Arena

Even more than infrastructure, nations emerging from conflict need better institutions. In most cases, these institutions need to be refashioned, not just rebuilt, since it was the old institutions that failed in the first place.
—James Dobbins (2007, 24)

Efforts to create a legitimate and community-oriented police force cannot succeed unless they take place in the context of an overall effort to enact Security Sector Reform (SSR). The term refers to a relatively new concept that covers the highly political and complex task of transforming the institutions and organizations responsible for dealing with security threats to the state and its citizens. The UN defines the security sector as the collective "structures, institutions, and personnel responsible for the management, provision, and oversight of security in a country" (UN Secretary General 2008, 5). Its definition includes those institutions concerned with defense, law enforcement, corrections, intelligence, border management, customs, civil emergencies, and the courts and tribunals that adjudicate cases of criminal conduct. Also included are institutions responsible for the management and oversight of security, such as the executive, ministerial, and legislative bodies of government, as well as civil society groups. Nonstate actors such as tribal leaders and other traditional authorities, militias, and private security services are also included. For the UN, SSR in particular is "a process of assessment, review, and implementation as well as [of] monitoring and evaluation led by national authorities that has as its goal the enhancement of effective and accountable security for the state and its people without discrimination and with full respect for human rights" (UN Secretary General 2008, 6).

Not everyone completely accepts the UN's definition of SSR, and there are heated debates over what institutions and activities should and shouldn't be included in the reform process. There are also questions about SSR's most effective application. SSR can be used as a tool for conflict prevention and conflict management, but the greatest attention has been focused on its applicability to postconflict reconstruction. After repeated failures, it is increasingly acknowledged that foreign interventions that stop at the training and equipping of indigenous security forces are unlikely to succeed. Instead, a comprehensive, whole-of-government approach is required on the parts of both the donor countries and the host government if simultaneous reform of all the institutions, both military and civilian, that are involved in providing security is to occur. The goal is a safe and secure society that enjoys good governance and operates under the rule of law (McFate 2008).

Along with the UN, the Organization for Economic Cooperation and Development (OECD), through its Development Assistance Committee (OECD-DAC), has emerged as a leader in the field of SSR. The OECD's policy on SSR was endorsed in April 2004 at a ministerial meeting of its thirty member countries, including the United States. Subsequently, the policy was spelled out in a widely accepted handbook that has been used as the basis for the SSR policies of most Western governments. According to the handbook, the basic approach for an effective SSR process includes: (1) local ownership with a basis in democratic norms, human rights, and the rule of law; (2) a whole-of-government approach involving both donor and host nation agencies as well as civil society; (3) a broad assessment of the full range of the security and justice-based needs of the population and the state; (4) the basic principles of good governance, including transparency and accountability; and (5) enhancement of the human capacity required to ensure institutions, once reformed, continue to function in an effective and just manner (Organization for Economic Cooperation and Development 2007).

Of these principles, the most important is ensuring the host country concurs with and is involved in SSR efforts. The stated objective in all peace and stability operations is to transfer responsibility for maintaining security from international forces to local military and police forces as quickly as possible. This cannot be done effectively, however, unless competent leadership is in place and violence and illicit wealth are no longer the determining factors in political outcomes. The timing of the transition to local authority and its success must be conditioned upon the willingness and the capacity of domestic institutions to govern in accordance with the rule of law and with the general consent of the population (Hartz, Mercean, and Williamson 2005).

Local ownership can be difficult to secure because SSR has the potential to change existing power relationships and threaten vested interests. It involves a wide range of local actors who may have conflicting perspectives and priorities. There may also be a lack of both human capacity and financial and material resources at the local level. The lengthy time horizon for SSR inevitably produces problems with donor coordination and donor fatigue. Major donors may be diverted by new crises or new priorities and lose interest before local institutions are ready to assume full responsibility for security (McFate 2008). One of the most import principles for international donors in SSR programs is to do no harm, closely monitoring events to ascertain that initiatives do not produce unintended consequences. Donors must ensure that assistance programs reduce rather than aggravate tensions and that they do not empower warlords, extreme nationalists, or other undemocratic forces.

Effective SSR requires coordinated assessment, planning, capacity building, implementation, and evaluation. Multidisciplinary teams that represent all the participating institutions, governments, and agencies should conduct comprehensive assessments of the defense and justice sectors. Coordinated, strategic planning should follow to ensure the inclusive and balanced development of the entire security sector. Since SSR is a comparatively new field, this effort will require training for those who are already engaged in SSR-related activities as well as local officials and security personnel. Both the ability to create a broader awareness of the nature and importance of SSR and the capacity to improve effectiveness are key to successful reform. Implementation will require the alignment of programs with an eye toward obtaining the goals and objectives outlined in the strategic plan, notwithstanding the different and often competing priorities, mandates, laws, and regulations of international and local agencies. Finally, continued monitoring and evaluation are necessary to ensure that SSR remains on track. Those who conduct program evaluations at key decision points and at the conclusion of specific projects should focus on the ends in order to gauge the effectiveness of the means.

SSR is essential to the transformation from conflict to sustainable economic progress and democratic government. Controlling, professionalizing, and rightsizing the security sector helps sustain peace by demilitarizing society and breaking the cycle of violence. Reform of the state's defense and police institutions frees resources that can then be used for poverty reduction and improved social welfare. SSR turns the security apparatus of the state from a competitor for resources into a partner for development and political reconciliation. Institutional reform of critical oversight agencies—that is, the defense and interior ministries and the intelligence services—instills norms of democratic governance and prevents regression once the intervention force has withdrawn. The end goal of SSR is a conflict-free, democratic state that operates under the rule of law and can attract foreign investment and participate effectively in the global community (Ferguson 2004).

Justice Sector Reform

Successful SSR is dependent upon a simultaneous and robust effort to develop the entire criminal justice system. At the outset of many peace and stability operations, state judicial systems are often literally in ruins, as they were in Somalia, Iraq, and Afghanistan. There, police were either unavailable or unwilling to serve or their service was unacceptable to the population. Courthouses and detention centers were destroyed. Law books and legal codes were lost. Judges, prosecutors, and court administrators had either disappeared or were too intimidated to come forward. Police are important to the restoration of public order and the rule of law, but they cannot function effectively without the other two parts of the so-called justice triad, courts and prisons. Functioning democracies require that those arrested be brought before judicial authorities before they are remanded to detention. Ultimately, they must appear before a competent judge in a court for trial; if convicted, they must be incarcerated in a penal facility that meets international standards and is staffed by trained corrections officers. Without a functioning judicial and penal system, the restoration of public order and the process of establishing the rule of law are seriously compromised (Perito 2004). In situations where the development of courts and prisons is insufficient or nonexistent and secure facilities in which to hold and try criminals are lacking, police face the invidious choice of punishing the miscreants themselves or letting them go. Either choice will demoralize and corrupt even the best-trained police force, severely undermine public confidence, and hobble efforts to establish democratic governance (Dobbins 2008).

One of the first issues to be addressed in conducting judicial reform is the question of which laws will be applied by the criminal justice system. Judicial and police training and law enforcement are dependent upon a clear body of applicable law. The US Constitution dates from 1789, but crisis states often adopt a series of constitutions and basic laws over the course of regime change. The status of this supposedly fundamental document may be open to question or elicit political tension, with various groups favoring one version over another. A country may also have competing legal systems. The continuum may begin with traditional or tribal codes and continue through religious laws of different faiths to formal legal codes adopted by governments that held power during various periods. Simply obtaining copies of legal documents may be a problem. The destruction caused by civil war may have included the burning of parliamentary buildings, courthouses, libraries, and government archives. Copies of the legal codes may have been destroyed or lost—assuming they were ever made at all, as is especially unlikely if the previous regime ruled by presidential or emergency decrees. There may also be peace treaties, international human rights standards, security council resolutions, and other legal instruments that must be taken into consideration (Dobbins et al. 2007).

In Afghanistan, the Bonn Agreement, which was signed by representatives of the Afghan people on December 5, 2001, established an interim authority to run the country. The Bonn Agreement reinstated the provisions of the 1964 constitution, formally returning the country to the judicial system that had existed in the New Democracy era between 1964 and 1973. The lack of courts and the absence of trained judges, lawyers, and court administrators, however, meant that much of the country has remained subject to local authorities. The issue of applicable law was also ambiguous, since the 1964 constitution had been superseded by a series of new constitutions and basic laws imposed by various regimes, including the Communist government that held power during the Soviet intervention. The Bonn Agreement recognized all Afghan laws that were consistent with international standards—but many of the laws adopted during the Taliban era were not. In Afghanistan, applicable law included a mix of customary law, *sharia* (Islamic) law, and state law that overlapped in some cases but was inconsistent in others. In the absence of clarity about the applicable law, judges and village councils applied their own versions of state law, traditional codes, or *sharia* law in settling disputes or determining retribution for crimes (Thier 2004).

In nearly all peace and stability operations, efforts to determine applicable law and rebuild the judiciary and penal systems have received far less attention and resources than has police reform. The creation of a fair and efficient judicial system necessitates the involvement of international personnel with expertise in everything from the construction and protection of secure courthouses to the education and training of judges, magistrates, prosecutors, defense attorneys, and court administrators. In some cases, international jurists may have to be pressed into service, as they were in Kosovo, because of intimidation of local personnel, endemic corruption, or a lack of public confidence. The same is true of rebuilding both jails for initial detention and prisons for long-term incarceration. Corrections reform should be done by specialists in jail and prison construction, prison management, and prisoner security. It should involve professional trainers in areas ranging from the intake and screening of detainees to the rehabilitation of those who have been convicted and sentenced. There is also a need for experts in the establishment of programs for prisoners' release, probation, and reintegration into the community (Perito, Dziedzic, and Cole 2004). Police should not handle corrections since they do not generally have the proper training and may lack the detachment to treat prisoners objectively.

The failure to rapidly develop effective courts and humane corrections facilities can create situations like the one that existed in Iraq in December 2008. As a result of the US failure to assign priority to and allocate resources for the construction of Iraqi courts and the training of Iraqi judicial personnel, the understaffed and ill-equipped Iraqi judicial system could adjudicate only a fraction of the cases of detainees. The Central Criminal Court of Iraq, which was established by the Coalition Provisional Authority (CPA) in 2003 as the flagship of Iraq's criminal justice system, had a large backlog of cases and failed to meet international standards of due process. According to Human Rights Watch, after long stays in pretrial detention, central court trials for accused insurgents relied on the testimony of secret witnesses and on confessions obtained under duress. Other Iraqi courts fared even less well in terms of providing rapid and fair trials (Human Rights Watch 2008). At the same time, the formal Iraqi prison system, although managed in a manner reasonably consistent with international standards, was unable to accommodate even the relatively small number of criminals that were convicted by the Iraqi courts (Detwiler 2008).

In camps with infamous names like Abu Ghraib, US military authorities held 23,000 Iraqi security detainees in June 2008. These prisoners were kept for extended periods without judicial review on accusations that they were involved in insurgent activity. Detainees ranged from those who were motivated by money or manipulation to ideological irreconcilables. The US-Iraq Status of Forces Agreement required that US-held prisoners be transferred to Iraqi custody. On December 2, 2008, the UN expressed grave concern about the 24,000 security detainees already in Iraqi detention facilities, noting serious cases of overcrowding, mistreatment, and other human rights violations (Associated Press 2008). Amnesty International warned that Iraqi detainees held by the United States would be at risk of torture or even execution if they were handed over to the Iraqis, noting that those already held by the Iraqis were kept in appalling conditions and subjected to routine abuse (Amnesty International 2008). The result of this impasse was a potential threat to the future stability of Iraq. Thousands of Iraqi citizens could not be detained indefinitely. Eventually, most security detainees will have to be returned to society, with no assurance that some will not again engage in terrorism or otherwise attempt to seek revenge for their incarceration.

Ministerial Reform

The most critical and most often neglected subject of justice sector reform is the bureaucratic agency responsible for the police and other internal security forces. In Iraq, as in previous peace and stability operations, the United States went directly about the task of training indigenous police with little or no thought given to the interior ministry, the institution to which the police would report. The imperative to put boots on the ground was felt to be far more pressing than the reform of the ministry that would supervise, manage, equip, and support the personnel wearing those boots. In some cases, it was assumed that the host government, the UN, or coalition partners would take care of such institutional reform, in others that the State Department or the Justice Department would provide the necessary funding and programs. In fact, neither the international community nor the US government had the expertise, experience, funding, or interest needed to reform an institution that was closely identified with the host government's sovereignty. At the same time, the host government was often unwilling or unable to challenge the powerful interests that moved quickly to seize control of an institution that not only controlled the police but often had responsibility for border control, local government, and other critical functions. As a result, newly minted police officers emerged from US training programs only to find themselves subservient to an institution that was dysfunctional at best and under the control of corrupt leaders with their own political agendas at worst (Hylton 2002).

The critical nature of ministerial reform and the disastrous consequences of the failure to achieve it are evident in the history of US involvement with the Iraqi Interior Ministry (MOI). From the intervention in 2003 to the signing of the US-Iraqi Status of Forces Agreement in 2008, the Iraqi MOI provided a negative case study.

How Could This Happen?

In December 2006, the Iraq Study Group reported that the MOI was rife with corruption, infiltrated by militia, and unable to control the Iraqi police. In July 2007, the *Los Angeles Times* reported that the MOI had become a "federation of oligarchs," and various floors of the building were controlled by rival militia groups and organized criminal gangs. The report described the MOI as an eleven-story powder keg of factions where power struggles were settled by assassinations in the parking lot (Parker 2007). In its September 2007 report, the congressionally mandated Independent Commission on the Security Forces of Iraq described the MOI as dysfunctional, sectarian, and ineffective—a ministry in name only (2007, 86). Even Interior Minister Jawad al-Boulani called for the comprehensive reform of his own ministry.

Despite its problems, the MOI was responsible for providing policy guidance, training, and administrative support for Iraq's four civilian security services. The Iraqi Police Service is a 275,300-member force, controlled at the provincial level to provide basic police services throughout the country. With 32,389 members, the Iraqi National Police is a gendarmerie that was deployed in Baghdad and other parts of the country to assist US and Iraqi military forces in counterinsurgency operations. The Iraqi Border Enforcement Service stations its 38,205 officers at strong points along Iraq's borders; they are charged with preventing infiltration, smuggling, and illicit trafficking. And the Facilities Protection Service (FPS), with a 150,000-member force of largely autonomous units, is responsible for protecting government ministries. In total, the MOI was responsible for an armed force of nearly 500,000 members—roughly three times as large as the Iraqi army, navy, and air force combined. It was also responsible for assorted civil functions such as issuing passports, immigration control, and the regulation of private security companies. How did this severely troubled but extremely critical institution come into being?

From the Backwater to the Frontline

In April 2003, with looters on the streets and fires burning in government buildings in Baghdad, the US military issued a call for Iraqi police officers to return to duty. On April 14, joint patrols of Iraqi police and American soldiers made their first appearance on the streets of the capital. Under the CPA, most of Iraq's military and civilian internal security agencies were disbanded. The MOI and the Iraqi police survived, but their senior leadership and middle management were dismissed when the CPA purged members of the Baathist party from the government. On July 13, the CPA appointed a twenty-five-member Iraqi Governing Council; Nouri Badran was named the minister of the interior. Six deputy ministers, representing the major Shiite, Sunni, and Kurdish parties, were also appointed to ensure no political faction gained control of the ministry (Rathmell 2007).

The MOI was reorganized and assigned new responsibilities. The Department of Border Enforcement was created to handle customs, immigration, and border patrol, tasks that previously had been undertaken by the army or other ministries. The CPA was unable, however, to provide the hundreds of international advisers that the US State and Justice Departments believed were needed to facilitate the expansion and train Iraqi personnel. Through massive recruitment, frontline police positions were filled and staff for new institutions such as the immigration service and border guard force were hired as the United States continued to pressure the MOI to rapidly train, equip, and deploy tens of thousands of new Iraqi police. Goals such as hiring 30,000 new policemen in thirty days were announced and implemented with little regard for the quality or vetting of candidates (Inspectors General 2005, 19). A report by the Special Inspector General for Iraq quotes then–Secretary of State Colin Powell and the commander of US forces in Iraq, Lieutenant General Sanchez, as stating that the US Defense Department inflated the number of Iraqi police and military forces while ignoring the fact that personnel quality was more important than quantity (Office of the Special Inspector General for Iraq Reconstruction 2009). The MOI was totally unprepared to conduct training for the massive influx of personnel. Training was limited to three weeks for former police officers, with most classes taught by US military police in police stations. As the insurgency took hold and security deteriorated, the goal for recruiting US police trainers and advisers to serve in Iraq plummeted from 6,500 to 1,500 to less than 350 by the spring of 2004 (US Department of Defense 2006, 101).

Revolving-Door Leadership Frustrates Progress

From 2003 to 2007, Iraq had four national governments and five different interior ministers. This revolving-door leadership only amplified the confusion generated by unrestrained growth in the number of police and the impact of the insurgency. On April 16, 2004, the CPA instituted a new federalism, transferring powers to provincial governments in what had traditionally been a highly centralized state. CPA Order 71 decentralized authority over police in Iraq, giving provincial governors responsibility for recruiting and supervising the Iraqi Police Service (Coalition Provisional Authority 2004). Minister of Interior Badran opposed this action, pointing out that the provinces were unprepared for the responsibility and that it was uncertain who would control police in various parts of the country. When his protests were ignored, Badran resigned and was replaced by a technocrat, Samir al-Sumaydi. Al-Sumaydi had no police experience, but he was a skilled administrator with a vision for reforming the MOI. In his two months in office, al-Sumaydi tried to put in place measures to improve management practices. He established a vetting procedure for the ministry's leadership, created an inspector general, and supported militia demobilization. Unfortunately, he had neither the political support nor the time in office to make lasting changes in the ministry (Rathmell 2007).

In June 2004, the CPA transferred sovereignty to the Iraqi Interim Government. Under a new prime minister, Ayad Allawi, who appointed a new interior minister, Falah al-Naqib. In his nine months in office, al-Naqib worked with General David Petraeus, then the Multi-National Security Transition Command–Iraq commander, to increase rapidly the number of Iraqi police. Al-Naqib also sought to provide the MOI with effective Iraqi constabulary forces following the poor performance of the police in battles against Shiite cleric Moqtada al Sadr's Mahdi Army. Al-Naqib created commando units comprised of former soldiers from elite units like Saddam's Republican Guard. These units were commanded by al-Naqib's uncle—Adnan Thabit, a former army general—and were personally loyal to the minister. The commandos were raised under MOI control, without the involvement of the United States or its Civilian Police Advisory Training Team. Despite initial misgivings, the US military provided arms and logistical support to these units, which proved effective under Minister al-Naqib's stewardship in fighting alongside US forces against Sunni insurgents and Shiite militia.

On January 30, 2005, the United Iraqi Alliance, a coalition of Shiite political parties, won elections for the Iraq National Assembly.

Ibrahim al-Jaafari became prime minister; Bayan Jabr, a member of the Supreme Council for the Islamic Revolution in Iraq, was named interior minister. The victorious parties, particularly Jabr's, saw the MOI as a prize. The Defense Ministry was under US military control, and US soldiers were embedded with Iraqi Army units. The MOI had only a small number of foreign advisers and security forces that were under Iraqi control. Minister Jabr used his position to place members of the Badr Brigade—his party's militia—in key positions in the ministry and in the commando units, where they replaced Sunnis (Independent Commission on the Security Forces of Iraq 2007). After the terrorist bombing of the Shiite al-Askari Mosque in Samarra on February 22, 2006, police commando units were used to terrorize, torture, and kill Sunnis and conduct ethnic cleansing.

On December 15, 2005, elections were held for a permanent Iraq National Assembly. It was not until May 20, 2006, however, that Iraqi politicians formed a new government. Nouri al-Maliki became prime minister; Jawad al-Boulani was named to head the MOI. Al-Boulani, a Shia and former air force engineer, had no political base, but he did have a reputation for administrative competence. He was given three powerful deputies from the Dawa, Badr, and Kurdish factions to ensure that no single party would control the MOI (Rathmell 2007). Al-Boulani publicly acknowledged the problems in the MOI and called for reform of the ministry and the removal of sectarian factions from the police. The United States transitioned its MOI advisory team from the State Department to the Civilian Police Advisory Training Team, forming a 100-member Ministry Transition Team of military and civilian advisers to help improve operations. In April 2006, the Multi-National Security Transition Command–Iraq (MNSTC-I) persuaded MOI to combine all of the police commando units into a single organization and called it the Iraq National Police. In October, the US military began a purge of all INP units that were involved in sectarian violence, arresting their leaders and subjecting the rank and file to vetting and training (also known as *re-bluing*) in civilian police skills.

In December 2006—the "Year of the Police," as it was proclaimed by the US military—ended with the announcement that MNSTC-I had met its target of training and equipping 187,800 police and border patrol agents. The achievement was quantitatively impressive, but the reality behind the numbers was troubling. Neither the US military nor Iraq's interior ministry could account for the number of trainees that had actually joined the police, the number of police serving, or what had happened to the uniforms, weapons, and equipment that had been issued to training center graduates (Inspectors General 2005). Anecdotal reports abounded of former trainees selling their sidearms and uniforms on the black market and returning to their militia units or private life. As we have seen in earlier chapters, autonomous provincial police chiefs hired personnel without the knowledge of the MOI or inflated budgets with lists of ghost officers whose salaries they pocketed. Despite the appointment of a new minister, Shiite militia continued to exert undue influence over all aspects of the MOI's operations. The ministry also continued to suffer from widespread corruption and experienced severe shortfalls in planning, program management, personnel, procurement, logistics, communication, and maintenance.

Despite these problems, the MOI was given a major new responsibility. On December 27, 2006, Prime Minister al-Maliki ordered the MOI to exert control over the estimated 150,000 members of the Facilities Protection Service, which guarded ministries, public buildings, and essential infrastructure in Iraq (Independent Commission on the Security Forces of Iraq 2007). The political parties that controlled the various government ministries had been allowed to recruit security units that were armed and issued badges and police-style uniforms. These private armies were a source of patronage and a means of funding militia groups. Although the prime minister ordered the MOI to supervise, downsize, and retrain the Facilities Protection Service, this task was clearly beyond the capacity of an institution already overwhelmed by its existing responsibilities for nearly 200,000 employees and police personnel.

Misplaced Priorities and Political Rivalries Frustrate Reform

In 2006, Interior Minister al-Boulani and his coalition advisers began an earnest attempt to implement political and administrative reforms. Unlike other Iraqi ministries, which were controlled by a single political party, the MOI was controlled by political factions that pursued their own interests—but occasionally cooperated to improve institutional capacity. Al-Boulani, whose authority stemmed originally from his relationship with the prime minister, shared power with his politically powerful deputies, independent power brokers, and relationship networks that controlled various aspects of ministry operations. The minister attempted to reset the internal political balance among the

Dawa, Supreme Iraqi Islamic Council (formerly known as the Supreme Council for the Islamic Revolution in Iraq), and Kurdish factions by restructuring the ministry, combining departments and appealing for cooperation from political leaders in the government. These actions exacerbated internecine power struggles that occasionally turned deadly, since even relatively low-level positions controlled resources and patronage and provided opportunities to profit from corruption. The struggle for control within the MOI reflected the larger political struggle and the power balance in Iraqi society (Rathmell 2007).

This was evident on December 20, 2008, when al-Boulani rushed back to Baghdad from overseas travel, convened a press conference, and denounced the arrests of over thirty senior MOI officials, including several police generals. The officials were detained under orders from a judicial committee under the control of Prime Minister al-Maliki for allegedly aiding insurgents and organized criminals and supporting remnants of Saddam Hussein's Baath Party. Many of those arrested were Sunnis, provoking outrage from the largest Sunni bloc in Parliament. Al-Boulani told the press the charges were fabricated and the arrests were made for political reasons related to provincial elections scheduled for January 2009. Beyond Shiite-Sunni rivalry, al-Boulani's newly organized political movement, the Iraqi Constitutional Party, was preparing to challenge the prime minister's Dawa Party and its coalition partner, the Supreme Islamic Iraqi Council, in the Shiite-dominated south. Details of this episode remain murky, but observers concluded that it was part of a power struggle over assignments to critical posts in the interior ministry hierarchy (Parker and Hameed 2008; Raghavan and Mizher 2008).

Within MOI, political loyalty or intimidation trumped efficiency and professionalism, with all but a very few officials unwilling to challenge authority or to put the general good ahead of self-preservation. At the same time, the administrative reform effort made some progress. The MOI developed a small but growing cadre of trained professionals who understood modern administrative procedures and were working to improve the ministry's performance. There was noticeable improvement in the MOI's capacity for planning, budgeting, procurement, and personnel management. The ministry produced a strategic plan that would be synchronized with the budget process. Efforts by US advisers and Iraqi officials in the Internal Affairs Office resulted in the removal or reassignment of some criminal elements. Responsibility for control of the police academies and police training was transferred to the Iraqis, with international advisers playing a limited role. Nonetheless, after five years, the United States remained far from its goal of creating either an effective interior ministry or Iraqi police forces that could protect Iraqi citizens, prevent terrorism, and control violent crime (Sherman and Carstens 2008).

Essential Steps in Ministry Reform

The US failure to reform the MOI in Iraq was due in part to a lack of understanding of its institutional role and of the steps required to achieve such a goal. The United States does not have a comparable institution of government, nor does it have an agency that is dedicated to reforming the institutions of foreign governments. In Iraq and numerous other countries, the interior ministry is responsible for the policies, funding, and oversight of civilian law-enforcement organizations, including the constabulary, the police, border security, and special investigation units. In some countries, the MOI also has responsibility for prisons, immigration, and local governance, including provincial, municipal, and district administration. Leadership of these component organizations is assigned to appointees with specific technical expertise, but all rely upon the policy guidance, funding, and administrative support of the MOI. Dysfunction on the part of the interior ministry would make it difficult if not impossible to achieve even minimally acceptable performance from component organizations. The interior ministry should be based upon an appropriate legal foundation; operate pursuant to a clearly articulated mission; function in accordance with established administrative and operational policies; and employ competent, properly supervised personnel. Transforming an interior ministry requires a reasoned and informed process that involves assessment, strategic planning, technical assistance, training, and equipment donation and evaluation (Mayer 2009).

Assessing the Interior Ministry

A successful effort at ministerial reform in a postintervention state must begin with a comprehensive assessment of the interior ministry and its role in both the justice sector and the conflict. A multidisciplinary team of international experts, assisted by carefully selected local nationals, should undertake the assessment. It should be representative of the nations and international organizations taking part in the intervention and should include personnel from relevant ministries in both the donor countries and the host government, as the product of a joint assessment team is more likely to attract broad support than the work of a single organization. The broader the expertise and experience of the team members, the more likely it is that their assessment will identify critical needs and make useful recommendations; the team should have a range of competencies including civilian policing, public administration, management, public finance, governance, culture, and history. The assessment should examine the host country's security sector, determine how the police and the military relate to one another therein, and evaluate the possibility of future cooperation. There should be a discussion of the risks as well as the opportunities facing the international intervention force. There must be a sophisticated understanding of who will win and who will lose in the process, as security forces come to serve the public interest rather than the state or the political powers that be (Organization for Economic Cooperation and Development 2007, 42–56).

The assessment should be designed to obtain current information in the following broad categories (Mayer 2009):

1. The general environment within which the MOI is functioning, taking into account all factors relevant to accomplishment of its mission including:
    - A. The history and continuing effects of the recent conflict;
    - B. The national and cultural context within which the MOI functions, including all pertinent criminal justice–related issues;
    - C. An overview of the history of the MOI and its component organizations, including previous levels of public support and voluntary compliance with the criminal law and authorities;
    - D. The identity, length of service, and summary of qualifications of senior ministry officials;
    - E. A governmental organizational table depicting the position(s) superior to the MOI with direct responsibility for its performance; and
    - F. The conditions, organizations, or forces that could impede MOI development or reform.
2. The functions that have either been lawfully assigned to the MOI by the constitution or other organic authority or delegated thereto by senior authorities lawfully empowered to do so.
3. A review of the criminal code and the criminal procedural code to determine police powers relative to the courts. The review

should identify gaps in legislation that would be important for dealing with modern criminal activities such as official corruption, cybercrime, money laundering, terrorism, aircraft hijacking, and organized crime.

4. An evaluation of the extent to which the MOI is performing assigned functions, including an analysis of all causative factors of deficient performance in terms of:
   A. The existence and clarity of legal authority for assigned functions;
   B. The competency of ministerial leadership and management with respect to planning, organizing, supervising, directing, inspecting, coordinating, evaluating, and budgeting activities;
   C. The intergovernmental relationships with both superior authorities and other ministries and organizations that constitute and support the criminal justice system;
   D. The adequacy (in quantity and quality) of facilities, equipment, and supplies; and
   E. The competency of personnel at all levels below that of the senior ministry executives.

Prior to deploying, the leaders of the assessment team should be tasked with developing a brief plan that describes (1) the assessment's purpose and methodology, (2) the composition of the team, and (3) a schedule of pertinent meetings and events. All team members should receive copies of the plan and an orientation so that they are thoroughly familiar with the goals and methods of their mission. Since assessments are often rushed and superficial, leading to problems with the implementation of future assistance programs, the team members must be given enough time upon deployment to consult with relevant officials in the host government across a number of levels of government as well as in the police and the military. It is also important that they meet with both official and nonstate security and justice providers; in postconflict environments, sectarian militia, home guards, and private security forces may hold enough power to challenge or overwhelm state institutions. Too, they must consult with representatives of civil society who have an informed perspective, such as academics, journalists, and staffers of nongovernmental organizations. While it is unlikely that written records or statistical materials will be reliable or even available after the conflict and the period of authoritarian rule that preceded it, any documentation that does turn up may provide insights, if only to highlight the extent of the corruption and unauthorized activities of the previous regime (Organization for Economic Cooperation and Development 2007).

Strategic Planning to Assure a Common Vision

A multidisciplinary strategic planning team should be appointed to develop the ministry's mission statement and identify the means to achieve its goals. The team should include personnel from all relevant criminal justice sectors and agencies. It should work with multinational and local partners to ensure that its efforts are aligned with US, international, and local priorities. It should include functional specialists and regional or national experts who have an understanding of the operational context. Strategic planning will require the full commitment of those involved as well as of adequate resources. The team's first activity will be to review the assessment and develop an integrated understanding of resource availabilities and dynamics of the local, regional, and international context. The strategic planning team should seek to avoid time pressures, inadequate information, turf contests, and problems with technological interoperability. After an initial review, the team should move forward with the process of developing the strategic plan (US Joint Forces Command 2005).

Strategic planning is the process by which the ministry can visualize its future and undergo the operations necessary to achieve that vision. Three critical steps are required to prepare a strategic plan. The first is the aforementioned drafting of a mission statement that clarifies the host of issues present at the beginning of the planning process. Among the most important of these are the identification of the main objectives for which the ministry and its constituent components are responsible and of the major policy questions, key actors, supporting tasks, and potential challenges (Hawley and Skocz 2005). The second step involves a study of the ministry's internal environment, including an analysis of its strengths and weaknesses, potential barriers to progress, and major challenges that must be addressed. The third step involves an assessment of the external environment, particularly the opportunities and threats confronting the ministry: determine the political, economic, social, and technological context and the key stakeholders, from legislative and regulatory bodies to civil society groups (Bushnell and Halus 1992). This so-called SWOT (strengths, weakness, opportunities, and threats) process should generate a strategy for reform in its analysis of how the ministry can utilize its strengths, improve its weaknesses, capitalize on opportunities, and mitigate threats.

Technical Assistance and Training for Ministerial Functions

Implementation of the strategic plan requires a team of carefully chosen civilian advisers and trainers with expertise in the major areas of the ministry's operations. This team should be recruited on the basis of extensive specialized experience in law enforcement and security operations and their institutions. The team should be knowledgeable about the findings of the initial assessment and fully conversant with the elements of the strategic plan. They do not necessarily need to be from the United States. In fact, interior ministry reform is an area where Europeans have a distinct advantage, given their decades of experience in assisting nations that reformed their interior ministries in order to qualify for membership in the European Union (Serwer and Chabalowski 2008). The administrative approach followed by Europeans is often more appropriate than the US model in many parts of the world, because of the colonial or other historic relationships among countries. This is particularly true in countries that base their legal systems on the French model of civil law, including some in the Middle East. Indeed, the preconflict justice systems of both Iraq and Afghanistan were more akin to European models than to the US system.

The major areas for administrative reform will vary with the history, culture, and bureaucratic infrastructure of the interior ministry and its role in the conflict. Areas of intervention may include change management, internal control and accountability mechanisms, problem solving, communications, organizational design, corruption control, personnel management, and procurement tracking systems. The effort to enhance accountability may include the institution of human-resource reforms such as a disciplinary policy, codes of conduct, mechanisms for responding to citizens' complaints, autonomous internal inspection, improved supervisory practices, and merit recruitment and promotion. Improving community relations may require strengthening public information services, media training, and outreach to civil society (USAID 2005). A detailed discussion of the reforms that must be undertaken in each function is beyond the scope of this study. However, a representative list would include the following:

- *Command and control:* leadership, senior management, first-line supervision, policy and procedures, chain of command, and performance accountability at all organizational levels
- *Strategic planning and operations:* design and oversight of activities and reporting

- *Intelligence:* collection, analysis, assessment, and production of intelligence
- *Budget and programming:* planning, allocation of resources, operational expenses
- *Logistics:* infrastructure management, warehousing, inventories, uniforms and equipment, vehicles, fuel, weapons and ammunition
- *Procurement:* ordering, contracting, purchasing
- *Human resources:* personnel management, recruitment, assignment, training, compensation programs, career development, disciplinary actions
- *Public affairs:* public information, citizen education and outreach, media
- *Communications and information services:* telephones, computers, information management, operational information network administration and maintenance, data management and security
- *Inspector general:* prevention of abuse and corruption
- *Internal audit:* evaluation of the ministry's economy, efficiency, and effectiveness
- *Internal affairs:* review of citizen complaints, officer discipline, dismissals for cause

Evaluating Progress and Incorporating Findings

Among the primary challenges to institutional reform is objective and informative evaluation of the usefulness of assistance programs and the progress achieved toward institutional transformation. Optimally, there should be continuous monitoring whereby foreign program directors and local managers can adjust assistance programs and correct ineffective practices in order to conform to changing contexts and identified needs. Reviews should take place periodically and be designed to encourage adjustments in program implementation. They should be used as management tools to inform ongoing operations (thereby disproving the common complaint from hard-pressed staff that evaluations are a waste of time and scarce resources); at the end of a project, they should also be done in order to incorporate lessons learned and inform future programming. Among the major challenges to effective reviews and evaluations are high levels of staff turnover and poor record keeping, particularly at the beginning of the process, when systems are not in place and there is extreme pressure to speed implementation. It may also be difficult to ensure that the information gained from this effort is heeded in future.

The evaluation should measure progress against baseline data gathered in the original assessment and against the goals and objectives outlined in the strategic plan. Criteria for evaluation should include the *relevance* of the assistance and reform activity to the priorities established in the strategic plan; the *effectiveness* of the assistance and reform effort in achieving established goals; the *efficiency* demonstrated in achieving stated results, in both qualitative and quantitative terms; the *impact,* both positive and negative, of the changes produced in the intervention and postintervention periods; and the *sustainability* of the reforms and of the ability of the local government to fund them over the long term from its own resources. These criteria are detailed in guidelines for the evaluation assistance programs developed by OECD-DAC that can be incorporated into the terms of reference for a review (Organization for Economic Cooperation and Development 2007).

It is of overriding importance that reviews and evaluations focus on the results achieved rather than on the inputs and outputs of the programs undertaken. In Iraq, the US military carefully tracked the number of trainees entering and graduating from US-run training programs, the number of uniforms and amount of equipment issued, the number of vehicles delivered, and the amount of office furniture provided. Numbers were routinely reported without reference to whether the graduates actually entered on duty, whether they could perform police functions, or whether they were functioning as agents of sectarian conflict. In a similar manner, the work of US advisers at the Ministry of the Interior was evaluated in terms of the number of hours the advisers spent at the ministry rather than on the impact of their advice or the acceptance of their recommendations. In December 2006, the "Year of the Police" ended with the claim that the US assistance program had achieved success because the target number of 187,800 Iraqi trainees had passed through one of various US-provided police training programs. US advisers were credited with providing 100,000 hours of advisory service to ministry officials (US Department of State 2006).

Results can also be evaluated through surveys by small teams of experts according to specified performance indicators. Qualitative observation by competent observers is often less costly and allows judgments that cannot be made through numbers. The goal of US programs for ministry reform should be to change the objective of the police from defense of the state to providing security for citizens and their property. Evaluations should include multiple efforts to seek the opinions of individual citizens and civil society groups, particularly those that represent minorities, determining their views on the police and on the efficacy and fairness of their service to the community. Other signs of success are the replication of training programs by local authorities, routine maintenance programs and the replacement of used equipment, the implementation of procedures, and continued support by ministry leadership through personnel rotations.

The Role of the Adviser

Successful organizational transformation often depends upon the ability of ministerial advisers to convey recommendations for change in a manner acceptable to their local counterparts. According to the 2009 *Commander's Guidance to the MNSTC-I Advisors* to the MOI in Iraq, the mission of the Advisor Corps is to "develop the Iraqi institutional capability needed for good governance and to generate and sustain Iraqi Security Forces" (Multi-National Security Transition Command–Iraq 2009). US advisers are instructed to give their Iraqi counterparts "their best counsel and advice to raise personal and organizational capability" (Multi-National Security Transition Command–Iraq 2009). The guidance document reminds advisers that they are the coalition's public face, seen at the highest levels of the Iraqi government, and that their actions reflect directly upon MNSTC-I and impact the effectiveness of the US effort in Iraq. It points out that the adviser's goal is to "learn as well as seek to mentor, partner, and advise," concluding that advisers need to remain strategically and tactically aware of emergent trends and to keep their command informed (Multi-National Security Transition Command–Iraq 2009).

The MNSTC-I *Commander's Guidance* provides a useful introduction to the responsibilities of ministerial advisers in all peace and stability missions. To work effectively, foreign advisers in interior ministries must accomplish the following tasks (Consortium for Complex Operations 2009):

- *Establish a close personal relationship.* In crisis countries, particularly in the developing world, establishing personal relationships takes time. The adviser must tailor his approach to the person he is advising based upon local circumstances, taking advantage of opportunities to create rapport, trust, and confidence. This can mean sipping numerous cups of tea during hours of conversation on non–work related subjects in order to reach an understanding concerning backgrounds, interests, and values. Without establishing a personal relationship, an effective working relationship is impossible.

- *Understand the workings of the ministry and the host government.* The adviser must be conversant with the structure and function of the ministry and the host government. This includes awareness of informal power relationships, the importance of tribal or ethnic affiliations, legal restraints, traditions, and unspoken assumptions. As reform goes forward, local counterparts will expect advisers to be aware of recent developments, areas of progress, and current challenges. Advisers must have a detailed understanding of the position that their advisees hold and of their backgrounds, relationships to other officials, and authority to make and influence decisions.
- *Provide expertise and policy guidance.* Advisers must be technical experts in their field, but they must also be able to translate and adapt their knowledge and skills to local circumstances. In some cases, this may involve teaching advisees a skill or new method of operation, but more often it involves suggesting alternatives and providing options. Advisers must understand the political context of their advice and the consequences for host country officials of following their suggestions. Suggesting a course of action that leads to adverse consequences for advisees can set back the entire advisory mission.
- *Connect advisees with essential services.* One of the adviser's primary roles is to provide the host government official with access to information, administrative support, and contacts that would otherwise be unavailable. This function can range from giving briefings on the latest techniques in the field to providing a computer to arranging for teams of experts to visit the ministry and work with its staff. In conflict countries, advisers may feel the need to provide their counterparts with VIP protection or armored vehicles to prevent intimidation or assassination. Providing services is one way for the adviser to demonstrate his usefulness and dependability in order to build trust and confidence.
- *Coordinate with the intervention force.* The adviser must continually report to his or her command or organization on the situation in the ministry and the status of the advisee. This involves providing updates on decisions and actions taken by the ministry, new issues, personnel changes, the status of relationships among leading figures in the ministry, and important personal

issues of the host country official who is being advised. These reports will enable the intervention force to plan effectively, anticipate problems, and provide the appropriate assistance to its local partners. Attention to this aspect of the adviser's responsibility will ensure greater effectiveness on the part of both the adviser and the advisee.

The role of a ministerial adviser may seem straightforward, but the international experience in postconflict operations, particularly in Iraq and Afghanistan, is replete with examples of unsuccessful efforts and missed opportunities. Many advisers in those countries, particularly military officers, failed to understand that becoming an adviser means moving from the world of command to the world of influence. Foreign advisers, especially those working with senior officials, can neither give orders nor instruct those they are advising how things should be done. In some cases, even the use of the term "mentoring" is considered derogatory. Similarly, advisers should not try to impose Western models or replicate foreign institutions or practices without regard for local circumstances or cultural traditions. Recreating a model US police station in an Afghan city is unlikely to assuage the problems faced by the Afghan police. Advisers also may fail because they concentrate on grooming individuals rather than strengthening institutions, only to watch their advisees be replaced and the situation revert to the status quo ante. Missteps usually stem from a failure to determine the priorities of the host government and tap the wisdom of local officials whose insights could impact the success of the assistance program (Consortium for Complex Operations 2009).

One way of minimizing mistakes is to provide advisers with predeployment training tailored to their assignment. Few subject matter experts intuitively know how to mentor foreign officials without at least an introduction to basic principles and techniques. Unfortunately, they rarely receive any training prior to deployment, and little effort is made upon their return to determine the lessons learned. There are a number of topics that should be covered in any course aimed at preparing ministerial advisers to work effectively. Beyond lectures in the history, culture, politics, and economics of the country of assignment, the training course should cover the following subjects:

- *Cultural awareness:* recognizing cultural assumptions and biases
- *Interpersonal communication:* verbal, nonverbal, and interpreter-mediated

- *Exerting influence:* empathy versus sympathy, consensus building, respect and humility
- *Understanding power relationships:* formal, informal, illicit
- *Negotiation and mediation:* nonviolent dispute resolution
- *Problem solving:* interpersonal and institutional
- *Organizational development:* leadership, planning, implementation, evaluation
- *Transition to independent operations:* preparation for departure (Consortium for Complex Operations 2009)

Conclusion

SSR is the key to effective governance and to establishing the legitimacy of the state, whose public face the police are. If citizens have confidence that the police will protect them and provide emergency services, they are likely to be loyal to the state. Similarly, if they believe they can rely upon the judicial system to provide justice, they are likely to view the state as legitimate and worthy of their support. More important than the police and courts, however, are the institutions that stand behind them. The interior and justice ministries are essential to providing good governance. If the ministries that support the police and judges are instead dysfunctional, corrupt, or politicized, the police and the courts will have little chance of fulfilling their missions, which will in turn have a negative impact upon efforts to rebuild the state. Unfortunately, the United States has been slow to recognize the importance of SSR in peace and stability operations. It has paid even less attention to developing the capacity to conduct ministerial reform. The price of this failure, while largely unreported, has been high in both Iraq and Afghanistan.

8

Getting It Right: Recommendations for US Policy

In recent years, the lines separating war, peace, diplomacy, and development have become more blurred and no longer fit the neat organizational charts of the twentieth century. All the various elements and stakeholders working in the international area—military and civilian, government and private—have learned to stretch outside their comfort zone to work together and achieve results.

—US Secretary of Defense Robert M. Gates (2008)

Let us recall the question of the US Marine officer we introduced at the beginning of this book. He asked, "How should I have gone about training Iraqi police in a place where security had not been fully established, when insurgent attacks were still common and criminal gangs operated with impunity?" Our answer is that training for local police must serve the fundamental goal of foreign intervention—namely, the creation of a stable and effective government acceptable to its own people. Local police are the public face of government. They have unique capabilities in achieving the goal of good governance even when confronted by violence and insecurity. Recent experience in Iraq and Afghanistan, however, makes clear that the US government has failed to develop local police forces in ways that contribute to government legitimacy.

How can US missions of stabilization and reconstruction be improved so that stability, security, and effective governance are achieved? How should missions plan and implement programs for the appropriate use of the local police during peacebuilding? Do US peacebuilding organizations facilitate the development of foreign policing as they should? In other words, what kind of capacity building does the US government need to do during peacebuilding missions in order to reform and rebuild local police institutions?

In order to answer these questions, we begin by reviewing our conclusions about the role and training of local police in postconflict environments. These constitute the substantive agenda that US-led intervention forces must adopt. Then we make specific recommendations about the actions the United States needs to take in order to do so and describe the steps being taken toward implementation. Finally, we examine the strategic logic that any commander in a peacebuilding mission must employ to rebuild stable and effective governance in the face of ongoing violence.

The Police Role in Peacebuilding

If the purpose of intervention is the reconstruction of stable, effective, and democratic government, local police play a uniquely important role. Although foreign militaries as well as foreign police can suppress violence and prevent crime, they cannot win the allegiance of the population on behalf of the local government. Foreign security forces are outsiders; they will go home. Furthermore, military action, whether carried out by foreigners or locals, is a poor tool for winning hearts and minds because it is more destructive and less discriminating than police action and directed by remote commanders rather than by local citizens. Meanwhile, whether they want to or not, local police reflect the character and capacity of the government that is being reformed and reconstructed. Deployed among the people on a daily basis, the police show in concrete terms for whom and in what manner governmental power will be used.

Gaining legitimacy for the government is not only important for long-run political stability. It also increases the ability of government to deal with violence in all its forms: insurgency, terrorism, and violent crime. A cooperative public, siding with a new political order and its agents, can provide information about potential violence, its perpetrators, and its root causes. By winning hearts and minds, local police can gain vital information and create an environment inhospitable to people who want to foment violence.

In short, there are two reasons local police should be considered primary in developing legitimate local government: they can provide crucial information for dealing with violence and they can demonstrate to a skeptical public that the government is worth supporting. These effects are mutually reinforcing. People who consider the government legitimate will be more likely to cooperate with the police; public input that results in improving public safety increases the legitimacy of government. Without public support, both the control of violence and the stability of the government are at risk. Local police are more important to the goal of winning this support than any other set of security agents, domestic or foreign. The key to achieving said goal, meanwhile, is to deploy police so that they serve the security needs of individual citizens in three ways: by making themselves available to citizens, by responding effectively to their requests, and by exhibiting fairness in their actions. We call this core policing. It is what local police in peacebuilding contexts should be trained to do.

Gaining the support of local populations does not depend on becoming proficient in the technical skills of law enforcement. It depends on developing new orientations to the work itself—again, toward availability, responsiveness, and even-handedness. The architects of foreign peacebuilding missions have concentrated too much on teaching specific, largely Western, skills of public order and law enforcement. Police trainers on stabilization and reconstruction missions need to focus instead on correcting the mistakes that have alienated local populations from the police in the past. Without exception in countries where peacebuilding has been undertaken, the police have served the interests of elites rather than ordinary citizens and have acted illegally, abusively, and for personal gain. In short, correcting the faults of the past should become the imperative for police training in the future.

But the reform and reconstruction of local police will not be accomplished through training alone. Significant change in the operational character of the police does not bubble up, it percolates downward. It must be facilitated by the reform and reconstruction of the institutions responsible for directing, administering, and supporting not only the police but the entire justice system—prosecutions, courts, and corrections. Central to this undertaking are interior and justice ministries. Political factions must agree on the function and conduct of the justice system if reform is to occur. For the police, reform must involve nonpolitical administration; the professional management of budgets, personnel, and procurement; and the selection of leaders publicly committed to strong discipline, transparency, and accountability.

In order to improve the public perception of police, those in charge of ministerial reform and police training must seek to change operational behavior. The orientations of core policing must be more than philosophies, more than principles remembered; they must manifest themselves in the way police work. But rank-and-file officers cannot be expected to translate availability, responsiveness, and fairness into action on their own; they must be coached and supervised by management that makes their training in core policing meaningful. Here is the place where foreign advisers and field training officers can play a critical role in reaffirming attitudes, behaviors, and lessons introduced during training programs.

There are many challenges to the democratic reform of ministerial operations and police practice. The most important is the persistence and even increase in violence from insurgents, rebels, terrorists, kidnappers, narcotics peddlers, and criminals in postconflict environments. Violence inevitably diverts peacebuilders away from core policing and toward militarized defense. Precisely when core policing is needed the most, it is most likely to be marginalized. As we have seen in Iraq and Afghanistan, the police are trained as "little soldiers" and thrown into offensive operations against insurgent forces. This is the central dilemma of peacebuilding and the primary obstacle to the creation of legitimate governance in the face of extremist and criminal violence. We will return to this problem after examining the implications of our police analysis for changing the organization and management of US peacebuilding missions.

Lack of US Government Capacity

The fundamental reason for the failure of US efforts to stabilize and reconstruct justice sectors during peacebuilding is the dispersal of government responsibility. The creation of effective institutions of law enforcement and justice abroad requires the coordination of agents with three assets: expertise in criminal justice, a developmental perspective, and experience in foreign program management. Unlike European governments, which have powerful interior ministries and national police forces, the United States has a bureaucratic black hole resulting from the constitutional separation of powers between the executive and judicial branches of government and the delegation of most judicial and law enforcement functions to state and local government (Rosenau 2007). There is no federal law enforcement entity in Washington to provide assessments and strategic planning for stability operations, to represent this function in the government's interagency policy process, or to take responsibility for managing the justice and law enforcement components of US intervention.

It was for just this reason that President Bush gave responsibility for all aspects of intervention in Iraq and Afghanistan, including ministerial reform and police training, to the Department of Defense in 2004 and 2005, respectively. As a result, the US military has taken over missions that had been managed by civilian agencies in earlier operations—not out of a desire to expand its authority but because of the weakness of civilian counterparts. Effective integration of US government efforts is impeded by gaps in civilian institutional infrastructure. This is particularly true in the critical area of the rule of law, where the lack of a national police force and of the capacity to deploy federal judicial and corrections officials means that the United States must use commercial contractors to staff police and judicial contingents in peace and stability operations. Lack of federal government civilian counterparts inhibits cooperation with the UN, other international organizations, and allied governments in the field. The US military's overarching role and the concomitant lack of a robust and effective civilian component also severely restrict the willingness of humanitarian and relief agencies—that is, nongovernmental organizations—to work with the United States. These agencies argue that US military presence violates so-called humanitarian space and endangers civilian aid workers who rely for security upon their public image as impartial noncombatants.

The US Department of State, which is responsible for formulating and supervising foreign policy, has almost no expertise in justice management or law enforcement; it has assigned the oversight of US police contingents in peace and stability to the International Narcotics and Law Enforcement Bureau (INL). Currently, the INL has only one career law enforcement professional on its staff, which is otherwise composed of foreign service officers, civil servants, and support staff. The INL has, in turn, outsourced the recruitment, training, and support of US police contingents in peace and stability missions to commercial contractors. The INL's work consists for the most part in administering contracts for the work it sponsors abroad. The United States Agency for International Development (USAID), which is accountable to the Department of State, has the needed development experience abroad, but it lacks the justice and law enforcement expertise. This is a matter of agency policy, a legacy of the congressional abolition of the controversial Office of Public Safety in 1975 and the enactment of Section 660 of the Foreign Assistance Act, which prohibits the use of foreign assistance funding to train foreign police forces (US Congress 1961). Although USAID participates in programs that promote the rule of law and the transition to democratic government, it has been reluctant to reengage in foreign police training except where responsiveness to civil authority and relations with civil society are involved.

The US Department of Justice (DOJ) is the nation's law firm, the central agency for enforcing federal law. It is staffed by US attorneys, who prosecute cases in federal courts. It does not have responsibility for federal courts, which constitute a separate branch of government, and its responsibility for international relations is limited to enforcing US criminal statutes. The DOJ Office of International Affairs, for example, is primarily concerned with negotiating legal assistance agreements and managing the extradition of foreign criminals to the United States for trial (US Department of Justice 2009). The DOJ includes four major federal law enforcement agencies: the FBI; the Drug Enforcement Agency; the Bureau of Alcohol, Tobacco, Firearms, and Explosives; and the Marshals Service. Legislation, politics, bureaucratic habit, and lack of expertise restrict these agencies to dealing with the domestic impact of various types of organized crime. Federal law enforcement agencies are inadequately staffed and have little capability to strengthen crisis states or confront foreign insurgencies. Their officers normally do not wear uniforms, nor do they perform the broad range of policing functions that are common for state and local police forces (Gompert et al. 2008).

The DOJ does not have the capacity to build comprehensive foreign criminal justice systems in postconflict environments. Its criminal division has two small offices whose mission is to train indigenous police and prosecutors abroad. The International Criminal Investigative Training Assistance Program (ICITAP) has provided training for police in more than eighty countries, including Haiti, Bosnia, and Kosovo. ICITAP is totally dependent on the State Department for policy guidance and project funding and does not constitute a line item in the DOJ budget. In recent years, the State Department has all but excluded ICITAP from Afghanistan and Iraq. Meanwhile, the Office of Prosecutorial Development and Training appoints assistant US attorneys to serve as advisers to foreign governments and as rule-of-law officers on provincial reconstruction teams in Iraq (ICITAP 2009). Like ICITAP, it depends on the State Department for policy, guidance, and funding.

In addition to its inexperience with coordinating and supporting full-service justice sector operations nationally, the United States is unable to deploy appropriate civilian personnel to serve as facilitators of institutional reform and training. The quality of the advisers and trainers that have served in Iraq and Afghanistan as well as in earlier peace and stability operations has varied widely. Because the United States has no national police counterpart to the Royal Canadian Mounted Police or the French Police Nationale, no US advisers have worked in a ministry that had responsibility for managing a national police force. Among the advisers selected from state and local law enforcement agencies, few have held senior executive positions; most were junior patrolmen on municipal police forces, deputy sheriffs, or others who had served in small police departments in rural areas. In many cases, they were less experienced than the Iraqis and Afghans they were assigned to advise. They were often younger than their counterparts in societies that place great value on age, rank, and social status. US advisers therefore had difficulty relating to their older and higher-ranking counterparts on a personal level. Senior Afghan National Police generals, for instance, had more than thirty years of experience and had attended training programs in Russia and Central European countries. It was difficult for them to accept advice from US advisers who might have had, say, less than a decade of experience as a highway patrolman.

Personnel recruited by commercial firms on contract to the State Department, which account for the bulk of US justice sector advisers, were also handicapped by the fact they were not government officials and could not make decisions or speak on behalf of the United States (Nikita 2008; Pumphrey 2008). Furthermore, federal regulations limit the ability of the State Department to closely supervise the selection, training, and conduct of contract personnel. As a study by the RAND National Defense Research Institute for the Department of Defense pointed out, "Using contractors to perform niche services is unavoidable; using them to perform functions of critical national importance borders on dereliction" (Gompert et al. 2008, 309).

Assigning responsibility for ministerial reform and police training to the Defense Department also proved to be an inadequate solution. The Defense Department and the US military may be able to run a police and justice system temporarily using military police, courts martial, and tribunals, but that is a poor model for a justice system in an emerging democracy. Military officers who were assigned as advisers to the interior ministries in Iraq and Afghanistan knew little about the administration of justice and generally were asked to operate beyond the limits of their core competencies (Gompert et al. 2008). Occasionally, the US military could assign US Army Reserve officers or National Guard members who were senior law enforcement professionals in their civilian lives, but the number of such people was limited, and once they had served a tour—normally less than a year—they were not available for follow-up assignments. More often, Reserve and National Guard soldiers, often serving in civil affairs units, were junior officers or from the enlisted ranks.

Building US Government Capacity

Since 2004, the United States has taken the first tentative steps toward creating the capacity to put the lessons learned in Iraq and Afghanistan into practice. On the military side, the fundamental importance of US military participation in peace and stability operations was acknowledged in November 2005 in a Defense Department Directive titled *Military Support for Stability, Security, Transition, and Reconstruction (SSTR) Operations* (US Department of Defense 2005). The directive identified peace and stability operations as a core mission of the US military, of equal importance with the conduct of combat operations. The directive noted that proper planning and execution of the postcombat phase of operations was essential to achieving victory and the rapid withdrawal of U.S. forces. It instructed the US military to develop new skills for rebuilding indigenous institutions, including local police forces, correctional facilities, and judicial systems—and to work closely with civilian government agencies in so doing. Finally, it urged the creation of training programs that would equip military personnel to perform essential functions, such as policing, until they could be transferred to civilian authorities (US Department of Defense 2005).

To fill the civilian side of the black hole, President Bush signed a National Security Presidential Directive, NSPD-44, a month later, in December 2005, which assigned responsibility for planning and coordinating the activities of US government civilian agencies in postconflict interventions to the Secretary of State (US National Security Council 2005). The Office of the Coordinator for Reconstruction and Stability Operations (CRS) was established within the State Department and authorized to create a Civilian Reserve Corps (CRC) to assist the US military in peace and stability operations, among other things. During its first years of operation, Congress did not appropriate money for its programs and required its administrative costs to be paid out of the State Department budget. In October 2008, the president signed the *Reconstruction and Stabilization Civilian Management Act,* part of the *Duncan Hunter National Defense Authorization Act for 2009,* which provided legislative authority for the CRS and the CRC. Following its passage, the CRS began implementing a plan to provide the United States with a limited capacity to deploy police and other critical civilian elements relatively quickly at the outset of a peace and stability operation. CRC officers could be deployed unilaterally or as part of a multinational or UN force. The plan called for the creation of a three-tiered capacity that could be activated and deployed in stages.

The first tier, or Active Response Component (ARC), would consist of 250 newly hired federal government personnel with expertise in the development of civilian aspects of government who could deploy on twenty-four hours' notice. These first responders would be assigned to military commands or US embassies to provide special expertise and engage in the assessment and planning of missions. The second tier, or Standby Response Component (SRC), would be composed of 2,000 federal personnel who would be trained, equipped, and prepared to leave their regular jobs and deploy abroad within thirty to sixty days of assignment. These individuals would augment the ARC by providing additional expertise and manpower for mobile headquarters or regional teams. The ARC and the SRC could be activated by the State Department. The third tier, the aforementioned CRC, would be composed of personnel from state and local governments as well as members of the private sector who would sign contracts with the federal government agreeing to deploy abroad in response to a call for their services. When activated by a decision of the president, these civilian specialists would become temporary federal employees, with corresponding privileges and responsibilities. A majority of the CRC would be involved with rule of law; most would be police. Over time the CRC would grow to about 2,000 personnel. Police and other rule-of-law experts would constitute the largest number of participants in all three stages (Herbst 2007).

New Institutions and Personnel Requirements

The integration of US military efforts with those of civilian government agencies is essential for success in postconflict interventions. This has been the most important lesson learned in Iraq and Afghanistan. Stabilization and reconstruction are severely handicapped when there is no common strategy and the Defense Department commands a preponderance of personnel, financial, and material resources. The creation of the CRS and the development of the ARC and SRC, along with the projected CRC, are positive steps in that they concentrate responsibility for civilian development abroad during peacebuilding and begin to address the dearth of qualified personnel for such missions. But more, much more is needed in order for the United States to successfully tackle security sector reform during peace and stability operations. Efforts to create a CRC with a few hundred members fall far short of building the national capacity to field teams of effective justice sector personnel, namely constabulary, police, prosecutors, judges, and corrections officers. The United States needs the capability to deploy several thousand specialists in the civilian aspects of development to work alongside US military forces in postconflict interventions.

The fundamental obstacle to executive reorganization is the US government's failure to move beyond the institutional structures that were in place at the end of the Cold War. As the Project on National Security Reform notes in "Forging a New Shield," the sixty-year-old structures and processes of the national security system no longer help US leaders formulate coherent strategies for integrating hard and soft power to achieve national objectives (Project on National Security Reform 2008). The inability of the CRS to fulfill its responsibilities under NSPD-44 highlights the need for a new government agency dedicated to managing the civilian aspects of postconflict interventions. This agency would be empowered and staffed to conduct operations and coordinate the actions of civilian agencies, particularly in managing the justice and police components of security sector reform. Such an institution would have to be positioned within the executive branch of government and supported by Congress in a manner that would correct the institutional stovepiping and weak interagency cooperation that are endemic features of the US national security system. The Office of the Special Inspector General for Iraq Reconstruction has come to the same conclusion, pointing out that the lack of executive authority over interagency coordination was "at the heart of the failures in Iraq reconstruction" and that "in the US system, only the president has the decisive authority necessary to require interagency coordination for complex contingency relief and reconstruction operations" (2009, 341).

For these reasons, we believe that an entirely new agency is needed: a Stability Operations Agency. This agency would be mandated by Congress and located in the Executive Office of the President. Based on a whole-of-government approach, it would be responsible for developing policy and coordinating and directing the activities of all civilian agencies in peace and stability operations. Such an organization would be able to act on lessons that should have been learned from previous operations. Most important of all, it could grapple explicitly with the problem of balancing the needs of security, for locals as well as donors, against the requirements for democratic development.

The Stability Operations Agency would be modeled on the Office of the US Trade Representative (USTR), which is responsible for developing international trade policy and conducting trade negotiations with other countries. The USTR is a cabinet member and the president's principal adviser, negotiator, and spokesperson on trade issues. The USTR coordinates trade policy through the interagency structure and draws upon experts from other government agencies in staffing US delegations to trade negotiations. Some of these negotiations, like the World Trade Organization talks, require large delegations, repeated negotiating sessions, and years to reach agreements (US Trade Representative 2009). Based on its direct relationship with the president and bureaucratic position within the Executive Office of the President, the USTR enjoys the authority to formulate trade policy and direct the work of other government departments, each having its own bureaus or offices concerned with trade matters.

The new Stability Operations Agency would be led by a senior official of sufficient stature to merit a position in the president's cabinet. It would be permanently staffed by specialists with extensive experience in peace and stability operations. This reform would provide the United States with a federal cadre of skilled advisers and trainers in the critical areas of interior ministry reform and police development and would limit the need to outsource these activities to commercial contractors. Moreover, it would enable the government to develop policies and doctrines for stabilization, reconstruction, and security sector reform. It would also allow the government to develop and use standardized procedures and curricula for advising and training local officials and police, relieving advisers and trainers of the need to improvise based on personal experiences. Such an organization could guard against the recurrence of the failures of Iraq and Afghanistan, where the lessons from previous operations were ignored and where untrained and inexperienced personnel made unfortunate decisions when faced with terrorist violence from insurgents and criminal elements.

As with the office of the USTR, the Stability Operations Agency would not be expected to provide from its own staff all the expertise required to successfully coordinate and implement peacebuilding in postconflict environments. It would need to draw on the knowledge and experience of subject matter experts throughout the federal government—which means that contributing departments and agencies would themselves need to be prepared for their specialized supporting roles.

For the State Department, the CRS would continue to play its current role of working with regional bureaus and USAID to organize departmental participation in peace and stability operations. This is a critical piece of US postconflict interventions, since diplomacy and development are key components of an effective operation. In the justice sector, the obvious candidate to provide required expertise is the DOJ. It has more expertise in justice sector administration than do other departments, growing experience in operations abroad, and embryonic capacity in institutional development in the forms of ICITAP and the Office of Prosecutorial Development and Training. It also has the stature to deal with its foreign ministerial counterparts and extensive professional contacts throughout the world, especially in law enforcement (Bayley 2006).

As presently organized, however, DOJ cannot provide the depth of support needed for stability operations. This is a matter of tasking. It needs to develop a new division, headed by an assistant attorney general, that is devoted to justice sector development abroad. The division would have two primary tasks: (1) to recruit and train personnel for all three tiers of the CRC and (2) to formulate, manage, and evaluate programs for justice sector reform abroad. By concentrating responsibility in the DOJ, the federal government would have, for the first time, a consolidated budget and a dedicated administrative support system for the domestic component of security sector reform. Administrative support is especially important for the adequate documentation of program implementations and the results thereof. Perhaps most important of all, the division would provide a voice at high levels of the federal government for the importance of justice sector development in stability operations.

The Strategic Logic of Reconstruction amid Violence

The central dilemma of peacebuilding is that insurgency, terrorism, and criminal violence lessen the likelihood that international intervention forces and local governments can develop and deploy the kind of police force that could contribute most to overcoming these very challenges. This is true in part because there is little understanding of the advantages that a police force supported by the public can bring to political stabilization and violence prevention. For policymakers, mission commanders, local politicians, and even affected populations, violence foments violent responses by forces that can conduct offensive operations. And there is also the grim reality that core police cannot deploy operationally at risk of death. Indeed, in such conditions it would be irresponsible to do so. Core police must, at the very least, receive the skills and equipment to protect themselves against attack while remaining within a bubble of military protection in the form of fortified stations, defensive armament and equipment, and the support of military forces who may be called in as backup.

The initial temptation on the part of commanders faced with paralyzing violence is to use police as "little soldiers," capable not only of defending themselves but of carrying the battle to the enemy. This is a mistake, as we have seen in Iraq and Afghanistan. The military and the police have different comparative advantages, and the unique capacities of both must be developed and used as needed. The basic principle for stability operations is that the military should protect the police, freeing them up to do what only police can do—win the public for the government and hence the struggle against insurgent and terrorist violence. Planning for the deployment of core police should take place simultaneously with intervention. Initial units should be trained immediately so that they can be deployed whenever and wherever security conditions allow. In all likelihood, they will not be deployed simultaneously across an entire country but selectively, where risk has been minimized by military action. If the military cannot provide sufficient security to allow civil police to maximize their comparative advantage, then civil police should not be deployed.

Regardless of the degree of insecurity encountered in peacebuilding, governmental legitimacy is the objective, police its primary instrument, and military force its operational enabler. This paradigm applies also to counterterrorism and crime prevention. In counterterrorism, the threat to core policing comes from the attractiveness—sometimes the necessity—of using civil officers as covert agents for intelligence and disruption. Likewise, when violent crime becomes endemic, policymakers as well as the public expect the police to "get tough," forming SWAT teams and undercover attack squads to find and repress criminals. Whenever violence increases, core policing is likely to be deemphasized if not sidelined entirely. Yet in dealing with the challenge of insurgency, terrorism, and violent crime, police are primary—not in the sense that they should take the lead from the beginning, but in the sense that they can uniquely foster something no other security agency can, namely, public support. They do this by serving citizens individually, proving available, responsive, and fair.

In foreign interventions, this prescription highlights the purpose of intervention: the stabilization and reconstruction of government rather than pacification and exit. The fundamental mistake that the United States made in Iraq and Afghanistan was failing to understand that invasion would require stabilization and reconstruction in addition to regime change. Consequently, police development in both countries was always catching up to conditions rather than successfully shaping them.

Just as there is a continuum of insecurity, so there is a continuum of police function. At one end, there is core policing; at the other, regime policing. In core policing, police activity is initiated by individual citizens from the bottom up. In regime policing, police action is initiated by government from the top down. In the real world, of course, policing is never purely one or the other. Even in democratic countries, police must deal with a shifting mix of threats to individuals and threats to society, including its governmental structure. There are sound reasons for using the police against both kinds of dangers. But if the focus on generalized threats comes at the expense of responding to individual needs, police risk forfeiting their unique advantage.

In peacebuilding, there are usually four security services to be mixed and matched: foreign military, foreign police, local military, and local police. What is required is an intricate collaboration of these resources, combined according to different and varying threats to public safety. Policymakers and mission commanders, whether faced with insurgency, terrorism, or criminality, must learn that available, responsive, and fair policing—core policing—constitutes an asset that is easy to lose and hard to replace. In all three arenas, the role of the police is the same, though they may have to be supplemented or even replaced by the military in counterinsurgencies, covert agents in counterterrorism, or paramilitary police in criminal hot spots. Faced with these choices, policymakers and commanders must understand what could be lost by pushing police too far in the direction of regime policing. In peacebuilding, the separation of protection from service leads to authoritarianism. In self-governing democratic societies, the separation of protection from service undermines crime control and prevention. In both cases, the legitimacy of governance is at stake.

Acronyms

ANA	Afghan National Army
ANCOP	Afghan National Civil Order Police
ANP	Afghan National Police
ANPA	Afghan National Police Auxiliary
AP3	Afghanistan Public Protection Program
ARC	Active Response Component
ASF	Auxiliary Security Force
CERP	Commanders Emergency Response Program
CNPA	Counter Narcotics Police of Afghanistan
COIN	counterinsurgency
CPA	Coalition Provisional Authority
CPATT	Civilian Police Advisory Training Team
CRC	Civilian Reserve Corps
CRS	Coordinator for Reconstruction and Stability Operations
CSTC-A	Combined Security Transition Command–Afghanistan
DOD	Department of Defense
DOJ	Department of Justice
EGF	European Gendarmerie Force
EUPOL	European Union Police Mission to Afghanistan
FDD	Focused District Development
GAO	Government Accountability Office
HNP	Haitian National Police
ICITAP	International Criminal Investigative Training Assistance Program
IFOR	Implementation Force

INL	International Narcotics and Law Enforcement Bureau
INP	Iraqi National Police
IPMs	International Police Monitors
IPS	Iraqi Police Service
IPSF	Interim Public Security Force
IPTF	International Police Task Force
ISAF	International Security Assistance Force
ISG	Iraq Study Group
KPS	Kosovo Police Service
KPSS	Kosovo Police Service School
LOTFA	Law and Order Trust Fund for Afghanistan
MNF	Multinational Force
MNSTC-I	Multi-National Security Transition Command–Iraq
MOI	Ministry of the Interior
MTA	Military Technical Agreement
MUP	Yugoslav Interior Ministry Special Police Unit
NCO	noncommissioned officer
NTM	NATO Training Mission–Afghanistan
OECD-DAC	Organization for Economic Cooperation and Development–Development Assistance Committee
OHR	Office of the High Representative
ORHA	Office of Reconstruction and Humanitarian Affairs
PDF	Panamanian Defense Force
PNP	Panamanian National Police
POP	problem-oriented policing
PRT	Provincial Reconstruction Team
PTT	Police Transition Team
SCIRI	Supreme Council for the Islamic Revolution in Iraq
SNP	Somalia National Police
SRC	Standby Response Component
SSR	Security Sector Reform
TIP	Transition and Integration Program
UNITAF	United Task Force
UNMBIH	UN Mission in Bosnia and Herzegovina
UNMIK	UN Mission in Kosovo
UNOSOM	United Nations Operation in Somalia
USTR	US Trade Representative

Bibliography

Afghan Ministry of Interior. *National Internal Security Strategy*. Kabul: Islamic Republic of Afghanistan, September 2006.

Aizenman, N. C. "Afghan Crime Wave Breeds Nostalgia for Taliban." *Washington Post,* March 18, 2005.

Amnesty International. "Afghanistan: Police Reconstruction Essential for the Protection of Human Rights." March 12, 2003. http://www.amnesty.org/en/library/info/ASA11/003/2003.

————. "Iraq: Security Agreement Puts Detainees at Risk of Torture." November 27, 2008. http://www.amnesty.org/en/for-media/press-releases/iraq-security-agreement-puts-detainees-risk-torture-20081127.

Anbaki, S., et al. "Police Lack Training, Firepower in Fighting Insurgency." *USA Today*. October 25, 2004.

Andrews, E. L. "Aftereffects: Anarchy; Iraqi Looters Tearing Up Archaeological Sites." *New York Times,* May 23, 2003.

Aolain, F. N. *The Politics of Force: Conflict Management and State Violence in Northern Ireland*. Belfast: The Blackstaff Press, 2000.

Asia Foundation. *Afghanistan in 2006: A Survey of the Afghanistan People.* San Francisco: Asia Foundation, 2006.

Associated Press. "Lawlessness and Looting Spread in Baghdad." *New York Times,* April 11, 2003.

————. "UN: Grave Situation for Iraqi Detainees." December 2, 2008. http://www.msnbc.msn.com/id/28020821/.

————. "McChrystal: Job 1 Is Protect Civilians." June 25, 2009. http://www.military.com/news/article/mcchrystal-job-1-is-protect-civilians.html?col=1186032310810.

Australian Broadcasting Company. "60-pc of Helmand Police Use Drugs." February 18, 2009. http://www.abc.net.au/news/stories/2009/02/18/2495328.htm.

Australian Federal Police. "Program Curriculum for Pre-Deployment Training Program." Canberra, Australia. August 30, 2007. http://www.afp.gov.au/international/IDG/pre-deployment_training.html.

Bailey, M., R. Maguire, and N. Pouliot. "Haiti: Military-Police Partnership for Public Security." In *Policing the New World Disorder: Peace Operations and Public Security,* edited by R. Oakley, M. Dziedzic and E. Goldberg, 215–252. Washington, DC: National Defense University Press, 1998.

Bair, A., and M. Dziedzic. "Bosnia and the International Police Task Force." In *Policing the New World Disorder: Peace Operations and Public Security,* edited by R. Oakley, M. Dziedzic, and E. Goldberg, 253–314.Washington, DC: National Defense University Press, 1998.

Baker, J., and L. Hamilton. *Iraq Study Group Report: The Way Forward—A New Approach.* New York: Vintage Books, 2006.

Baker, K. "Q and A with Afghan Leader Karzai." *Chicago Tribune*, December 21, 2008.

Bayley, D. H. *Patterns of Policing.* New Brunswick, NJ: Rutgers University Press, 1985.

————. *Police for the Future.* New York: Oxford University Press, 1994.

————. *What Works in Policing.* New York: Oxford University Press, 1997.

————.*Changing the Guard: Developing Democratic Police Abroad.* New York: Oxford University Press, 2006.

Bayley, D. H., and C. D. Shearing. *The New Structure of Policing: Description, Conceptualization, and Research Agenda.* Washington, DC: National Institute of Justice, 2001.

Bayley, D. H., and D. Weisburd. "Cops and Spooks: The Role of the Police in Counterterrorism." In *To Protect and Serve: Policing in an Age of Terrorism and Beyond,* edited by D. Weisburd, T. E. Feucht, I. Hakimi, L. F. Mock, and S. Perry, 81–100. New York: Springer, 2009.

BBC. "Iraqi Police Deaths Hit 12,000." *BBC News,* December 24, 2006.

Bensahel N., et al. "After Saddam: Prewar Planning and the Occupation of Iraq." RAND Monograph. Washington, DC: RAND Corporation, 2008.

Bittner, E. *The Functions of Police in a Modern Society.* Chevy Chase, MD: National Institute of Mental Health, 1970.

Borger, J. "Pentagon Warned Over Policing." *The Guardian,* May 28, 2003.

Bowden, M. *Black Hawk Down: A Story of Modern War.* New York: Atlantic Monthly Press, 1999.

Branigan, W., and R. Atkinson. "Anything, and Everything, Goes." *Washington Post,* April 12, 2003.

Brewster, M. "NATO Disbands Afghan Auxiliary Police." *The Canadian Press,* May 15, 2008.

Brinkley, J. "In Basra, Old Scores Settled at Gunpoint." *International Herald Tribune,* November 1, 2003.

Broadwell, P. "Iraq's Doomed Police Training." *Boston Globe,* August 30, 2005.

Bulloch, G. "Military Doctrine and Counterinsurgency: A British Perspective." *Parameters* (Summer 1996): 4–16.

Burack, J. "Policing in Kosovo: Putting Police Skills to Work in Police Operations." *Subject to Debate* 14, no. 2–3 (2000).

Bureau of Justice Statistics. *State and Local Law Enforcement Training Academies, 2006.* Washington, DC: US Department of Justice, 2006.

Burke, Gerald. "Iraq Experience Project." US Institute of Peace. October 8, 2004. http://www.usip.org/library/oh/iraq.html.

Burns, J. F. "Joint Patrols Begin in Baghdad." *New York Times,* April 14, 2003.

Bushnell D., and M. Halus. "TQM in the Public Sector: Strategies for Quality Service." *National Productivity Review* (Summer 1992): 355–370.

Call, C. "Institutional Learning with ICITAP." In *Policing the New World Disorder: Peace Operations and Public Security,* edited by R. Oakley, M. Dziedzic, and E. Goldberg, 315–364. Washington, DC: National Defense University Press, 1998.

Center for Strategic and International Studies. "Public Opinion in Iraq, November 2004." In *Progress or Peril? Measuring Iraq's Reconstruction,* edited by B. Crocker, 6–8. Washington, DC: CSIS, 2004.

Cha, A. E. "Crash Course in Law Enforcement Lifts Hopes for Stability in Iraq; Academy Set to Train a New Generation of the Country's Police." *Washington Post,* December 9, 2003.

Chalk, P. *West European Terrorism and Counter-Terrorism.* New York: St. Martin's Press, 1996.

Chapman, R., et al. *Local Law Enforcement Responds to Terrorism Lessons in Prevention and Preparedness.* Washington, DC: US Dept of Justice, Office of Community Oriented Policing Services, 2002.

Clarke, R. V., and G. R. Newman. *Outsmarting the Terrorists.* New York: Praeger Security International, 2006.

Coalition Provisional Authority. *Order Number 71: Local Governmental Powers.* Baghdad, Iraq: CPA, April 6, 2004.

Coalition Provisional Authority and Iraq Ministry of Interior. *Iraq Police: An Assessment of Their Present and Recommendations for the Future.* Baghdad, Iraq: CPA, May 30, 2003.

Cohn, E. S., and S. O. White. "Legal Socialization Effects on Democratization." *International Social Science Journal* 49 (1997): 151–171.

Commission on Presidential Debates. "The Second Bush-Gore Presidential Debate." October 11, 2000. http://www.debates.org/pages/trans2000b.html.

Connors, T. P., and G. Pellegrini. *Hard Won Lessons: Policing Terrorism in the United States.* New York: Manhattan Institute for Policy Research, 2005.

Consortium for Complex Operations. Ministerial Advising Workshop. Discussion on the role of US advisers in postconflict interventions. US National Defense University, February 10, 2009.

Consortium for Response to the Afghanistan Transition. "Filling the Vacuum: Prerequisites to Security in Afghanistan." International Foundation for Electoral Systems. March 2002. http://www.ifes.org/news/craft.pdf

Constable, P. "In Postwar Baghdad, a Benz Is Easy to Get, Easy to Lose; Theft of New and Luxury Cars Becomes Rampant in the Capital." *Washington Post,* August 10, 2003.

———. "Resistance to US Plan for Afghanistan." *Washington Post,* January 16, 2009.

Corum, J. S. *Training Indigenous Forces in Counterinsurgency: A Tale of Two Insurgencies.* Washington, DC: US Army Strategic Studies Institute, 2006.

CPATT. *Year of the Police: MOI/Police Capacity Building Workshop.* Executive Brief. Washington, DC: CPATT, September 27, 2006.

D3 Systems and KA Research Ltd. "Iraq Poll March 2008." *BBC News,* September 10, 2007. http://news.bbc.co.uk/2/hi/middle_east/6983027.stm.

Dagher, S. "How Much Safer Is Baghdad Now?" *Christian Science Monitor,* November 27, 2007.

Day, G. "After War, Send Blue Force." *Christian Science Monitor,* May 30, 2001. http://www.csmonitor.com/2001/0530/p11s2.html

Denham, T. "Police Reform and Gender." In *Gender and Security Sector Toolkit,* edited by M. Bastick and K. Valasek. Geneva: DECAF, UN-INSTRAW, OSCE-ODHIR, 2008.

Detwiler, E. "Iraq: Positive Change in the Detention System." USIP Peace Briefing, July 2008. http://www.usip.org/pubs/usipeace_briefings/2008/0723_iraq_detention.html.

Diamond, L. "What Went Wrong in Iraq?" *Foreign Affairs* 83, no. 5 (2004): 34–56.

Dobbins, J. *Nation-Building and Counterinsurgency After Iraq*. New York: The Century Foundation, 2008.

Dobbins, J., et al. *America's Role in Nation-Building: From Germany to Iraq.* Washington, DC: RAND Corporation, 2003.

————. *The Beginner's Guide to Nation-Building.* Washington, DC: RAND Corporation, 2007.

Dunford, David. "Iraq Experience Project." United States Institute of Peace, August 25, 2004. http://www.usip.org/library/oh/iraq.html.

Eck, J. E. *Solving Crimes: The Investigation of Burglary and Robbery.* Washington, DC: Police Executive Research Forum, 1982.

Eck, J. E., et al. *Problem Solving: Problem Oriented Policing in Newport News.* Washington, DC: Police Executive Research Forum, 1987.

Ellis, J. *From the Barrel of a Gun.* London: Greenhill Books, 1995.

Ellison, G., and J. Smyth. *The Crowned Harp: Policing Northern Ireland.* London, UK: Pluto Press, 2000.

Ferguson, C. "Police Reform, Peacekeeping and SSR: The Need for Closer Synthesis." *Journal of Security Sector Management* 2, no. 3 (2004): 1–13.

Finley, B. "Feds Turning to Local Police to Fight Homegrown Terror." *Denver Post,* August 25, 2006.

Freedberg, S. J. "Iraq Police Primer." *The National Journal* 43 (2003): 3265–3272.

Freeze, C. "For Afghan Police, Staying Alive Is the First Priority." *Globe and Mail,* January 14, 2008.

Galula, D. *Counter-Insurgency Warfare: Theory and Practice.* New York: Praeger, 1964.

Gates, R. "Remarks Before the U.S. Global Leadership Campaign." Washington, DC: US Global Leadership Campaign Tribute Dinner, July 15, 2008.

Gellman, B. "Seven Nuclear Sites Looted; Iraqi Scientific Files, Some Containers Missing." *Washington Post,* May 10, 2003.

Gilmore, Gerry. "Trainers Critical to Obama's New Afghan-Pakistan Plan, Mullen Says." US Department of Defense, March 27, 2009. http://www.defenselink.mil/news/newsarticle.aspx?id=53688.

Glanz, J., and D. Rohde. "Panel Faults US Trained Afghan Police." *New York Times,* December 4, 2006.

Goldsmith, A. "'It Wasn't Like Normal Policing': Voices of Australian Police Peace-keepers in Operation Serene, Timor-Leste 2006." In *Community Policing and Peacekeeping,* edited by P. Grabosky, 119–133. Boca Raton, FL: CRC Press, 2009.

Goldstein, H. *Problem-Oriented Policing.* Philadelphia: Temple University Press, 1990.

Gompert, D., et al. *War by Other Means.* Washington, DC: RAND Corporation, 2008.

Gordon, M. "US Planning to Regroup Armed Forces in Baghdad, Adding to Military Police." *New York Times,* April 30, 2003.

———. "The Strategy to Secure Iraq Did Not Foresee a Second War." *New York Times,* October 19, 2004.

Gordon, M., and B. E. Trainor. *Cobra II: The Inside Story of the Invasion and Occupation of Iraq.* New York: Vintage Books, 2003.

Government of Germany. Closed Session Briefing, National Defense University, September 16, 2002. Attended by the author.

Gow, J. *Triumph of the Lack of Will: International Diplomacy and the Yugoslav War.* New York: Columbia University Press, 1997.

Gray, A., and M. Manwaring. "Panama: Operation Just Cause." In *Policing the New World Disorder: Peace Operations and Public Security,* edited by R. Oakley, M. Dziedzic, and E. Goldberg, 41–68. Washington, DC: National Defense University Press, 1998.

Grayling, A. C. "Drying Out the Insurgency." *New York Times,* March 27, 2006.

Greenwood, P. F., J. Petersilia, and J. Chaiken. *The Criminal Investigation Process.* Lexington, MA: D. C. Heath, 1977.

Hansen, A. *From Congo to Kosovo: Civillian Police in Peace Operations.* London: International Institute for Strategic Studies, 2002.

———. "The EUPM in Bosnia-Herzegovina: Achievements and Prospects." Unpublished manuscript. Geneva: 2003.

Hansen, W., T. Gienanth, and R. Parkes. "International and Local Policing in Peace Operations." In *Report of the 8th International Police Workshop.* Berlin: Center for International Peacekeeping (ZIF), 2006.

Harman, D. "How US Tries to Limit Civilian Deaths in Afghanistan." *Christian Science Monitor,* January 13, 2009.

Hartz, H., L. Mercean, and C. Williamson. "Safeguarding a Viable Peace: Institutionalizing the Rule of Law." In *Quest for a Viable Peace: International Intervention and Strategies for Conflict Transformation,* edited by J. Covey, M. Dziedzic, and L. Hawley, 157–204. Washington, DC: US Institute of Peace Press, 2005.

Hawley, L., and D. Skocz. "Advance Political-Military Planning." In *Quest for a Viable Peace: International Intervention and Strategies for Conflict Transformation,* edited by J. Covey, M. Dziedzic, and L. Hawley, 37–76. Washington, DC: US Institute of Peace Press, 2005.

Henry L. Stimson Center. *Security in Afghanistan: The International Security Assistance Force.* Peace Operations Backgrounder. Washington, DC: Henry L. Stimson Center, June 2002.

Herbst, J. *Stabilization and Reconstruction Operations: Learning from the Provincial Reconstruction Team (PRT) Experience.* Testimony of the Coordinator of Reconstruction and Stabilization, 110th Cong., 1st Sess., October 30, 2007. http://www.house.gov/hasc/calendar_past_hearings.shtml.

Hines, L. G. "Iraq Experience Project." United States Institute of Peace, October 3, 2004. http://www.usip.org/library/oh/iraq.html.

Hoey, B. (Lt. Col), Spokesman for IFOR. Press Briefing, April 27, 1996. http://www.nato.int/ifor/trans/t960427a.htm.

Hoffman, B. *Insurgency and Counterinsurgency in Iraq.* Santa Monica, CA: RAND Corporation, 2004.

Holbrooke, R. *To End a War.* New York: Random House, 1999.

Holland, J., and S. Phoenix. *Phoenix: Policing the Shadows.* London: Hodder and Stoughton, 1996.

Howard, P. *Hard Won Lessons: How Police Fight Terrorism in the United Kingdom.* New York: Manhattan Institute for Policy Research, 2004.

Human Rights Watch. "Hearts and Minds: Post-War Civilian Deaths in Baghdad Caused by US Forces." 15, no. 9E (2003). http://www.hrw.org/reports/2003/iraq1003/.

———. "The Quality of Justice: Failings of Iraq's Central Criminal Court." New York, NY: Human Rights Watch. December 2008.

Hylton, J. "Security Sector Reform: BiH Federation Ministry of the Interior." *International Peacekeeping* 9, no. 1 (2002): 153.

Independent Commission on Policing in Northern Ireland. *A New Beginning: Policing in Northern Ireland.* Belfast: Her Majesty's Stationery Office, 1999.

Independent Commission on the Security Forces of Iraq. *The Report of the Independent Commission on the Security Forces of Iraq.* Washington, DC: Independent Commission on the Security Forces of Iraq, 2007. http://www.csis.org/files/media/csis/pubs/isf.pdf.

Inspectors General, US Department of State and US Department of Defense. *Interagency Assessment of Iraqi Police Training.* Department of State Report no. ISP-IQO-05-72. July 15, 2005. http://www. oig.state.gov/documents/organization/55371.pdf.

———. *Interagency Assessment of Afghanistan Police Training and Readiness.* Department of State Report No. ISP-IQO-07-07, Department of Defense Report No. IE-2007-001, November 2006. http://www.dodig.osd.mil/inspections/Index.htm.

International Crisis Group. Kosovo Report Card. ICG Balkans Report. 100, August 28, 2000. http://www.crisisgroup.org/home/index.cfm?id=1587&l=1.

———. "Reforming Afghanistan's Police." Policy Report. August 31, 2007. http://www.crisisgroup.org/home/index.cfm?id=5052.

Iraq Body Count. www.iraqbodycount.org/database.

Jalali, A. "The Future of Security Institutions." In *The Future of Afghanistan,* edited by J. A. Thier, 23–34. Washington, DC: United States Institute of Peace Press, 2009.

Jehl, D. "As Order Breaks Down, Allies Try to Rebuild Iraqi Police." *New York Times,* April 12, 2003.

Johnson, C. Jr. "Afghanistan Security, US Efforts to Develop Capable Afghan Police Forces Face Challenges and Need a Coordinated, Detailed Plan to Help Ensure Accountability." Statement before the House Committee on Oversight and Government Reform Subcommittee on National Security and Foreign Affairs. June 18, 2008. http://nationalsecurity.oversight.house.gov/story.asp?ID=2006.

Jones, J. L., and T .R. Pickering. *Afghanistan Study Group Report*. Washington, DC: Center for the Study of the Presidency, January 30, 2008.

Jones, S. "Averting Failure in Afghanistan." *Survival* 48, no.1 (2006): 111–128.

————. *Counterinsurgency in Afghanistan*. Washington, DC: RAND Corporation, 2008.

Jones, S., et al. *Securing Tyrants or Fostering Reform? US Internal Security Assistance to Repressive and Transitioning Regimes*. Washington, DC: RAND Corporation, 2006.

Joulwan, G. A., and C. C. Schoonmaker. *Civilian-Military Cooperation in the Prevention of Deadly Conflict: Implementing Agreements in Bosnia and Beyond*. New York: Carnegie Corporation of New York, 1998.

Kahl, C. H. "COIN of the Realm." *Foreign Affairs* 86, no. 6 (2007): 169–176.

Kaplan, D. E. "The Spy Next Door." *U.S. News and World Report,* May 5, 2006, 41–49.

Kelly, R. "American Law Enforcement Perspectives on Policing in Emerging Democracies." In *Policing in Emerging Democracies: Workshop Papers and Highlights*. Report of the National Institute of Justice Workshop on Policing in Emerging Democracies, Washington, DC, December 14–15, 1995.

Kilcullen, D. J. "Counterinsurgency Redux—A Report from the Field." Unpublished report. Washington, DC, 2006.

Kitson, F. *Low Intensity Operations: Subversion, Insurgency, Peace-keeping*. Harrisburg, PA: Stackpole Books, 1971.

Kovchok, E. "Kosovo Police Service Trainers." *Law and Order Magazine,* March 2001.

Kozak, M. Interview at the State Department Haiti Working Group, Washington, DC, February 3, 2000.

Kratcoski, P. C. "Police Education and Training in a Global Society: Guest Editor's Introduction." *Journal of Police Practice and Research* 5, no. 2 (2004): 103–105.

Kurtz-Phelan, D. "The Long War of Genaro Garcia Luna." *New York Times Magazine,* July 13, 2008.

Latin American Public Opinion Project. *Survey from July 2006*. The Americas Barometer (LAPOP), 2007. http://www.LapopSurveys.org.

Legon, A. "Ineffective, Unprofessional and Corrupt: The Afghan National Police Challenge." Foreign Policy Research Institute, June 5, 2009. www.fpri.org/enotes/200906.legon.afghannationalpolice.html.

Leiby, R. "For Crime Victims in Iraq, No Place to Turn." *Washington Post,* May 12, 2003.

Levitz, S. "Afghan Police Still Weak Link in Effort to Secure Afghanistan." *Canadian Press,* June 10, 2007.

Loeb, V., and B. Graham. "Groups Say US Lags on Restoring Order." *Washington Post,* April 12, 2003.

Lonaway, K. A., S. Welch, and L. F. Fitzgerald. "Police Training in Sexual Assault Response: Process, Outcomes, and Elements of Change." *Criminal Justice and Behavior* 28, no. 6 (2001): 695–730.

London Metropolitan Police Service. *Communities Together: A Guide to Best Practice*. London: London Metropolitan Police Service, 2006.

Lunney, R. F. "The Next Big Thing." *Blue Line Magazine* (June–July 1998): 1–24.

Lynch, C. "Afghan Opium Production Falls, Despite Problem Provinces." *Washington Post,* August 27, 2008.

Lyons, W. "Partnerships, Information and Public Safety: Community Policing in a Time of Terror." *Policing: An International Journal of Police Strategies and Management* 25, no. 3 (2002): 530–542.

Magnier, M., and S. Efron. "Arrested Development on Iraqi Police Force." *New York Times,* March 31, 2004.

Maguire, E. R. and W. R. King. "Federal-Local Coordination in Homeland Security." In *Security and Justice in the Homeland: Criminologists on Terrorism,* edited by B. Forst, et al. Paper presented at the annual meeting of the American Society of Criminology, unpublished anthology manuscript, May 24, 2009.

Malin, M. *U.S. Civil-Military Imbalance for Global Engagement.* Washington, DC: Refugees International, 2008.

Marenin, O. "Changing Police, Policing Change: Towards More Questions." In *Policing Change, Changing Police: International Perspectives,* edited by O. Marenin. New York: Garland Publishing, 1996.

———."The Role of Bilateral Support for Police Reform Process: The Case of the United States." *International Peacekeeping* 6, no. 4 (1999): 93–112.

Mastrofski, S. D., and R. R. Ritti. "Police Training and the Effects of Organization on Drunk Driving Enforcement." *Justice Quarterly* 13, no. 2 (1996): 291.

Mayer, R. Interview with Special Advisor to the Bureau of International Narcotics and Law Enforcement, Department of State, Washington, DC, January 29, 2009.

McFate, S. "Securing the Future: A Primer on Security Sector Reform in Conflict Countries." Washington, DC: US Institute of Peace, Special Report no. 209, September 2008.

McVey, P. M. *Terrorism and Local Law Enforcement: A Multidimensional Challenge for the Twenty-First Century*. Springfield, IL: Charles C. Thomas Publisher, 1997.

Miller, L., and R. Perito. "Establishing the Rule of Law in Afghanistan." Washington, DC: US Institute of Peace, Special Report no. 117, March 2004.

Monk, R. *End-of-Mission Report of the Seventh Police Commissioner of the United Nations International Police in Kosovo and the Kosovo Police Service, March 2007–February 2008.* Pristina, Kosovo: UNMIK, 2008.

Moss, M. "Law and Disorder: How Iraq Police Became Casualty of War." *New York Times,* May 22, 2006.

Moss, M., and D. Rohde. "Law and Order: Misjudgments Marred US Plans for Iraqi Police." *New York Times,* May 21, 2006.

Multi-National Security Transition Command–Iraq. *Commander's Guidance to the MNSTC-I Advisors.* Baghdad, Iraq: CENTCOM, January 5, 2009.

Murney, T., and J. McFarlane. "Police Development: Confounding Challenges for the International Community." In *Policing and Peacekeeping,* edited by P. Grabosky, 201–230. Boca Raton, FL: CRC Press, 2009.

Murray, T. "Police-Building in Afghanistan: A Case Study of Civil Security Reform." *International Peacekeeping* 14, no.1 (2007): 108–126.

Nagl, J. A. *Counterinsurgency Lessons from Malaya and Vietnam: Learning to Eat Soup with a Knife.* Westport, CT: Praeger, 2002.

Neil, R. R. "From National Security to Citizen Security: Civil Society and the Evolution of Public Order Debates." Unpublished manuscript, 1999.

Neild, R. *Policing Haiti: Preliminary Assessment of the New Civilian Security Force.* Washington, DC: Washington Office on Latin America, 1995.

Nelson, S. S. "US Helps Afghans Assume Control of Local Security," National Public Radio, *Morning Edition,* June 2009.

Nelson A. Rockefeller Institute of Government. *The Role of "Home" in Homeland Security: The Federalism Challenge.* Albany, NY: Nelson A. Rockefeller Institute of Government, 2003.

Nikita, J. Interview with former senior UN police adviser to the Afghan Ministry of Interior, Washington, DC, 2008.

NOETIC Corporation. *International Transitional Law Enforcement Environment: TLE Capabilities for International Operations.* Washington, DC: NOETIC Corporation, 2008.

Oakley, R., M. Dziedzic, and E. Goldberg. *Policing the New World Disorder: Peace Operations and Public Security,* Washington, DC: National Defense University Press, 1998.

Office of the High Representative and EU Special Representative. "General Framework Agreement for Peace in Bosnia and Herzegovina," Annex 11 (International Police Task Force). Article I. Paris: OSCE, 1995. http://www.oscebih.org/overview/gfap/eng/.

———.*Agreement on Restructuring the Police, Federation of Bosnia and Herzegovina.* Bonn: OHR, 1996. http://www.ohr.int/other-doc/fed-mtng/default.asp?content_id=3576.

Office of the Special Inspector General for Iraq Reconstruction. *Hard Lessons: The Iraq Reconstruction Experience.* February 2009, 333–341. http://www.sigir.mil/hardlessons/Default.aspx.

O'Hanlon, M. E. *The Role of State and Local Governments in Homeland Security.* Washington, DC: US Senate and Brookings Institution, 2005.

Oppel, R., Jr. "Corruption Undercuts Hope for Afghan Police." *New York Times,* April 8, 2009. www.nytimes.com/2009/04/09/world/asia/09ghazni.html.

Organization for Economic Cooperation and Development. *The OECD DAC Handbook on SSR: Supporting Security and Justice.* Paris: OECD, 2007. http://www.oecd.org.dac/conflict/if-ssr.

Organization for Security and Cooperation in Europe. "Kosovo Police Service School." *Details Newsletter* 2, no. 5 (June 2005): 1–12. http://www.osce.org/publications/mik/2005/06/15193_410_en.pdf.

Oversight Commissioner. *Reports.* Belfast, Northern Ireland: Office of the Oversight Commissioner, 2000–2007.

Pagon, M., et al. "European Systems of Police Education and Training." In *Policing in Central and Eastern Europe: Comparing Firsthand Knowledge with Experience from the West,* edited by M. Pagon, 551–574. Slovenia: College of Police and Security Studies, 1996.

Paley, A. R. "Attacks in Baghdad Kill 13 US Soldiers in 3 Days." *Washington Post,* October 5, 2006.

Parker, N. "The Conflict in Iraq: A Ministry of Fiefdoms." *Los Angeles Times,* July 30, 2007.

Parker N., and S. Hameed. "Iraq Releases Detained Security Officers." *Los Angeles Times,* December 20, 2008.

Perito, R. "The Experience of ICIAP in Assisting the Institutional Development of Foreign Police Forces." Paper delivered at the 35th Annual Program of the Academy of Criminal Justice Sciences. Albuquerque, New Mexico, March 10–14, 1998.

————. *The American Experience with Police in Peace Operations.* Clementsport, Canada: Pearson Peacekeeping Press, 2002.

————. *Where Is the Lone Ranger When We Need Him? America's Search for a Postconflict Stability Force.* Washington, DC: US Institute of Peace, 2005.

————. "The Coalition Provisional Authority's Experience with Public Security in Iraq." Washington, DC: US Institute of Peace, Special Report no. 137, April 2005.

————. "Policing Iraq: Protecting Iraqis from Criminal Violence." Washington, DC: US Institute of Peace, Peace Briefing, June 2006.

————. "Reforming the Iraqi Interior Ministry, Police and Facilities Protection Service." Testimony Before the House Armed Services Subcommittee on Oversight and Investigations. Washington, DC: March 2007.

Perito, R., M. Dziedzic, and E. Cole. "Building Civilian Capacity for US Stability Operations." Washington, DC: US Institute of Peace, Special Report, no. 118, April 2004.

Peterson, J. "More Than 12,000 Iraqi Police Casualties in 2 Years." *CNN World Service,* October 7, 2006.

Petraeus, D. H. "Learning Counterinsurgency: Observations from Soldiering in Iraq." *Military Review* (January–February 2006): 1–12.

Pfaff, T. *Development and Reform of the Iraqi Police Forces.* Carlisle, PA: US Army War College, Strategic Studies Institute, 2008.

Pirnie, B. R., and E. O'Connell. *Counterinsurgency in Iraq (2003–2006).* Washington, DC: RAND National Defense Research Institute, 2008.

Project on National Security Reform. "Forging a New Shield." Center for the Study of the Presidency, 2008. http://www.pnsr.org/data/files/pnsr_forging_a_new_shield_report.pdf.

Pumphrey, R. Interview with former senior UN police adviser to the Iraq Ministry of Interior, Washington, DC, 2008.

Raghavan, S., and Q. Mizher. "Government Offers Contradictory Explanations for Interior Ministry Detentions." *Washington Post,* December 19, 2008.

Rathmell, A. "Fixing Iraq's Internal Security Forces: Why Is Reform of the Ministry of Interior So Hard?" Washington, DC: Center for Strategic and International Studies, 2007.

Reuters. "US Troops Urged to Halt Anarchy in Baghdad." *New York Times,* April 11, 2003.

Richman, D. "The Right Fight: Enlisted by the Feds, Can Police Find Sleeper Cells and Protect Civil Rights, Too?" *Boston Review* 14 (2004–2005): 29–35.

Ricks, T. E. "De Facto Police Chief Hits Streets of Baghdad; US Military Encourages Iraqi Patrols in Capital." *Washington Post,* May 23, 2003.

Rieff, D. "Blueprint for a Mess." *New York Times,* November 2, 2003.

Riley, K. J., et al. *State and Local Intelligence in the War on Terrorism.* Santa Monica, CA: RAND Corporation, 2005.

Rosenau, W. "Little Soldiers: Police, Policing, and Counterinsurgency." Unpublished manuscript, 2007.

Rule, S. *Public Opinion on National Priority Issues, March 2000.* Pretoria, South Africa: HSRC Press, 2000. http://www.hsrcpress.ac.za/product.php?productid=1951.

Runge, J. W. "Traffic Law Enforcement and Homeland Security." In *Homeland Security: Best Practices for Local Government,* edited by R. L. Kemp, 45–48. Washington, DC: International City/County Management Association, 2003.

Sarway, B. "Bribery Rules on Afghan Roads." *BBC News,* July 7, 2008.

Schmitt, E., and D. E. Sanger. "Aftereffects: Reconstruction Policy; Looting Disrupts Detailed US Plan to Restore Iraq." *New York Times,* May 19, 2003.

Schultz, R., Jr. *In the Aftermath of War: US Support for Reconstruction and Nation Building in Panama Following Just Cause.* Maxwell Air Force Base: Air University Press, 1993.

Sedra, M. "Security Sector Reform and State Building in Afghanistan." In *Afghanistan: Transition Under Threat,* edited by G. Hayes and M. Sedra, 193–196. Waterloo: Wilfrid Laurier University Press, 2008.

Sepp, K. I. "Best Practices in Counterinsurgency." *Military Review* (May–June 2005): 8–12.

Serwer, D., and M. Chabalowski. "Shifting to Multilateralism." *The International Herald Tribune,* November 23, 2008.

Shadid, A. "A City Freed from Tyranny Descends into Lawlessness." *Washington Post,* April 11, 2003.

———. "In Searching Homes, US Troops Crossed the Threshold of Unrest." *Washington Post,* May 30, 2003.

Sheridan, M. B. "Police Force Is an Experiment in Rebuilding." *Washington Post,* April 16, 2003.

Sherman, M. Interview with the adviser to the Tenth Mountain Division. Washington, DC, June 19, 2009.

Sherman, S., and R. Carstens. "Cooling the Streets: Institutional Reforms in Iraq's Ministry of Interior." Report by the Institute of the Theory and Practice of International Relations, The College of William and Mary, Williamsburg, VA, November 14, 2008.

Skogan, W., and K. Frydl, K. *Fairness and Effectiveness in Policing: The Evidence.* Washington, DC: National Academies Press, 2004.

Skolnick, J. H., and D. H. Bayley. *Community Policing: Issues and Practices Around the World.* Washington, DC: National Institute of Justice, 1989.

Slevin, P., and B. Graham. "US Military Spurns Postwar Police Role." *Washington Post,* April 10, 2003.

Smith, R. J. "Kosovo Still Seethes as UN Official Nears Exit." *Washington Post,* December 18, 2000.

————. "Now for Nation Change. Law and Order: The Military Doesn't Do Police Work. Who Will?" *Washington Post,* April 13, 2003.

Spearin, C. "Assessing the Relationship Between Humanitarian Actors and Private Security Companies." In *Private Actors and Security Governance,* edited by A. Bryden and M. Caparini, 234–245. New Brunswick, NJ: Transaction Publishers, 2006.

Stephens, D. Interview, New York, November 19, 2008.

Struck, D. "National Police Force Sought in Afghanistan." *Washington Post,* February 5, 2002.

Sturcke, J. "Up to 150 Kidnapped from Baghdad Institute." *The Guardian,* November 14, 2006.

Swedish National Criminal Police. "Swedish Police Courses, Pre-Mission Training." Stockholm, Sweden: Swedish National Criminal Police, 2008.

Tavernise, S. "US and Afghan Forces Seize Biggest Drug Cache to Date." *New York Times,* May 24, 2009. http://www.nytimes.com/2009/05/24/world/asia/24afghan.html.

Thier, J. A. "Reestablishing the Judicial System in Afghanistan." Working Paper prepared for the Center on Democracy, Development and the Rule of Law, Stanford Institute for International Studies, no. 19. September 1, 2004. http://cddrl.stanford.edu/publications/reestablishing_the_judicial_system_in_afghanistan/

Thompson, R. *Defeating Communist Insurgency: The Lessons of Malaya and Vietnam.* New York: Praeger, 1966.

Tomes, R. R. "Relearning Counterinsurgency Warfare." *Parameters* (Summer 2004): 16–28.

Tonry, M. "Preface." In *Legitimacy and Criminal Justice: International Perspectives,* edited by T. R. Tyler, et al., 3–8. New York: Russell Sage Foundation, 2007.

Travis, J. *Inventory of State and Local Law Enforcement Technology Needs to Combat Terrorism.* Washington, DC: National Institute of Justice, 1999.

Trojanowicz, R., and B. Bucqueroux. *Community Policing: A Contemporary Perspective.* Cincinnati, OH: Anderson, 1990.

Tyler, T., and J. Fagan. *Report: Legitimacy and Cooperation: Why Do People Help the Police Fight Crime in Their Communities?* Report 06-99. New York: Columbia Law School, 2006.

Tyler, T. R., et al. "Legitimacy and Criminal Justice." In *Legitimacy and Criminal Justice: International Perspectives,* edited by T. R. Tyler, et al., 9–29. New York: Russell Sage Foundation, 2007.

UN Assistance Mission to Iraq. "Human Rights Report." 2007. http://www.ohchr.org/EN/Countries/MENARegion/Pages/UNAMIHRReports.asps.

UN Development Programme, Emergency Response Division. *UNDP Security Sector Reform Assistance in Post-Conflict Situations: Lessons*

Learned in El Salvador, Guatemala, Haiti, Mozambique, Somalia and Rwanda. Unpublished draft report.

UN Office on Drugs and Crime. *Global Report on Crime and Justice.* New York: Oxford University Press, 1999.

UN Office on Drugs and Crime and Afghan Ministry of Counternarcotics. *Afghanistan Opium Survey 2006.* New York: Oxford University Press, 2006.

UN Office on Drugs and Crime and Afghan Ministry of Counternarcotics. "Afghan Opium Survey 2008." Kabul, Afghanistan, August 2008. http://www.unodc.org/unodc/en/frontpage/opium-cultivation-in-afghanistan-down-by-a-fifth.html.

UN Security Council. *Security Council Resolution 794 [on the Situation in Somalia].* December 3, 1992. http://dacess-ods.un.org/TMP/7890062.html.

————. *Security Council Resolution 1244 [on the Situation Relating to Kosovo].* June 10, 1999. http://www0.un.org/Docs/scres/1999/sc99.htm.

————. *Security Council Resolution 1386 [on the Situation in Afghanistan].* December 20, 2001, S/RES/1386. http://www.un.org/News/Press/docs/2001/sc7248.doc.htm.

UN Secretariat. *Agreement on Provisional Arrangements in Afghanistan Pending the Re-establishment of Permanent Government Institutions.* 2001. http://www.unama-afg.org/docs/_nonUN%20%Docs/_Internation-Conferences&Forums/Bonn-Talks/bonn.htm.

UN Secretariat Department of Public Information. *The Blue Helmets: A Review of United Nations Peacekeeping.* New York: United Nations Publications, 1996.

UN Secretary General. *Report of the Secretary General on the Situation in Afghanistan and Its Implications for International Peace and Security.* S/2002/278-A/56/875. March 18, 2002: 9–12.

————. *Report on Securing Peace and Development: The Role of the United Nations in Supporting Security Sector Reform.* A/62/659-S/2008/39. January 23, 2008: 5–6.

US Army/US Marine Corps. *The U.S. Army/U.S. Marine Corps Counterinsurgency Field Manual.* Chicago, IL: University of Chicago Press, 2007.

US Congress. *Foreign Assistance Act of 1961.* 87th Cong., 1st Sess., 1961.

————. *Duncan Hunter National Defense Authorization Act of 2009. Title XVI: Reconstruction and Stabilization Civilian Management Act.* S. Rep. No. 3001, 110th Cong., 2nd Sess. 2008.

US Department of Defense. *Military Support for Stability, Security, Transition, and Reconstruction (SSTR) Operations.* Directive 3000.05. 2005. November 28, 2005.

————. *Measuring Stability and Security in Iraq.* Report to Congress in Accordance with the Department of Defense Appropriations Act (section 9010, Public Law 109-289). November 2006.

US Department of Interior. "Mission Statement." 2009. http://www.doi.gov/secretary/mission.html.

US Department of Justice. "Mission Statement." 2009. http://www.usdoj.gov/02organizations/.

US Department of State. *Iraq Weekly Status Report.* Washington, DC: US Department of State, December 20, 2006.

———. *Counterinsurgency for U.S. Government Policy Makers: A Work in Progress.* Washington, DC: US Department of State, 2007.

US Government Accountability Office. "Afghanistan Drug Control: Despite Improved Efforts, Deteriorating Security Situation Threatens U.S. Goals." Washington, DC: GAO-07-78, November 15, 2006.

———. "Securing, Stabilizing, and Rebuilding Iraq, Progress Report: Some Gains Made, Updated Strategy Needed." GAO-08-837, June 2008: 16.

———. "Afghanistan Security: U.S. Programs to Further Reform Ministry of Interior and National Police Challenged by Lack of Military Personnel and Afghan Cooperation." Washington, DC: GAO-09-280, 2009.

US ICITAP. "Mission Statement." 2009. http://www.usdoj.gov/criminal/icitap/.

US Institute of Peace, Security Sector Reform Working Group. "Policing Afghanistan: A Meeting of the Security Sector Reform Working Group." May 27, 2009. http://www.usip.org/events/2009/0527_policing_afghanistan.html.

US Joint Forces Command. "US Government Draft Planning Framework for Reconstruction, Stabilization, and Conflict Transformation." J7 Pamphlet, Version 1.0. December 1, 2005.

US National Security Council. *United States Government Operations in Iraq.* Presidential Decision Directive 36, Washington, DC, NSC. May 11, 2004.

US National Security Council. *Management of Interagency Efforts Concerning Reconstruction and Stabilization.* Presidential Decision Directive 44, Washington, DC, NSC. December 7, 2005.

US Park Police. "Mission Statement." 2009. http://www.nps.gov/uspp/.

US Senate Foreign Relations Committee. *Iraq: Assessment of Progress in Economic Reconstruction and Governmental Capacity.* Washington, DC: US Senate, 2005.

US Trade Representative. "Mission Statement." 2009. http://www.ustr.gov/Who_We_Are/Section_Index.html.

USAID. *Assistance for Civilian Policing: USAID Policy Guidance.* PD-ACG-022. Washington, DC: USAID. December 2005. http://dec.usaid.gov/index.cfm?p=express.issue&CFID=4408&CFTKEN=68197454&issueid=12.

Vennard, M. "US Afghan Tribe Plan Risky." *BBC News,* January 14, 2009.

Waldman, A. "After the War: Law Enforcement; US Struggles to Transform a Tainted Iraqi Police Force." *New York Times,* June 20, 2003.

Wardlaw, G. *Political Terrorism: Theory, Tactics, and Counter-Measures.* New York: Cambridge University Press, 1982.

Wasserman, R. "Remarks." Speech by the UN Deputy Police Commissioner, International Police Task Force, Contributors Meeting, Headquarters, United Nations, New York, June 26, 1996.

Wentz, L. *Lessons from Bosnia: The IFOR Experience.* Washington, DC: National Defense University Press, 1998.

Wilder, A. *Cops or Robbers? The Struggle to Reform the Afghan National Police.* Kabul: Afghanistan Research and Evaluation Unit, July 2007.

Williams, D. "American Copter in Collision Was Chasing Gunman; Cause of Crash in Mosul Still Unclear." *Washington Post,* November 17, 2003.

Wood, S. "Retraining Iraq Police Brigade Is Right Decision, General Says." *American Forces Press Service,* October 6, 2006.

Index

About the Book

Frustrated efforts in both Iraq and Afghanistan give urgency to the questions of how to craft effective, humane, and legitimate security institutions in conflict-ridden states—and whether legitimate policing can in fact be developed in the midst of insurgency and terrorism. David H. Bayley and Robert M. Perito confront these questions head on.

Against the backdrop of failed US attempts to train police forces in Iraq and Afghanistan, Bayley and Perito explore the role of the local police as an element of successful peace operations and counterinsurgency campaigns. Their analysis ranges from the specifics of training to the larger arena of broad institutional reform. Equally practical and grounded in theory, their work offers crucial guidance on the role and training of local police forces that must grapple daily with the challenges of ongoing conflicts.

David H. Bayley is distinguished professor in the School of Criminal Justice at the University at Albany, State University of New York. His numerous publications include, most recently, *Changing the Guard: Developing Democratic Police Abroad* and *What Works in Policing.* He is also author of the UN's program for community policing in the rebuilding and reform of police in peacekeeping operations. **Robert M. Perito** is senior program officer at the US Institute of Peace. He served as deputy director of the US Justice Department's International Criminal Investigative Training Assistance Program from 1995 to 2001, and from 1967 to 1995 he was a US Foreign Service officer, where his last assignment was director of the Office of International Criminal Justice. He is the author of *Where Is the Lone Ranger When We Need Him? America's Search for a Post-Conflict Security Force,* among many other works.